Making Sense

Margot Northey

Making Sense

third edition

a student's guide to

research, writing, and style

Toronto   OXFORD UNIVERSITY PRESS

Oxford University Press, 70 Wynford Drive, Don Mills, Ontario M3C 1J9

Toronto   Oxford   New York
Delhi   Bombay   Calcutta   Madras   Karachi   Kuala Lumpur
Singapore   Hong Kong   Tokyo   Nairobi   Dar es Salaam
Cape Town   Melbourne   Auckland   Madrid

and associated companies in
Berlin   Ibadan

This book is printed on permanent (acid-free) paper ⊖.

Canadian Cataloguing in Publication Data

Northey, Margot, 1940–
  Making sense

3rd ed.
Includes index.
ISBN 0-19-540938-8

1. Exposition (Rhetoric).   2. English language – Rhetoric.
3. Report writing.   I. Title.

LB2369.N67 1993   808'.042   C93-093180-7

Printed in Canada

Contents

Acknowledgements

In preparing the third edition of *Making Sense*, as in previous edtions, I have incorporated many suggestions from users in every part of the country. The enthusiasm of students and their instructors provided the impetus to keep improving. For all their comments I am grateful. I also appreciate the help of two former colleagues at University of Toronto, Dr. Margaret Procter and Lille Huggett. Martin Walker of Price Waterhouse made suggestions for the catchlist of misused words and phrases. For part of the material on word-processors, I want to thank Professor Brian Timney of the University of Western Ontario. Lynn McClary of the Western Business School handled many of the logistics in the revision process, including tidying up my typing. Finally, I am grateful for the assistance of Brian Henderson, Publisher at Oxford University Press, and for the astute editing of Sally Livingston.

Symbols for common errors

NOTE: If any of the following markings appear on one of your essays or reports, consult Chapter 9 or 10, or the Glossary, for help.

agr   agreement of subject and verb

amb   ambiguity

awk   awkwardness

cap   capitalization

cs   comma splice

dang   dangling modifier (*or* dm)

D   diction

gr   grammar (*or* usage)

mod   misplaced modifier

new paragraph

//   parallelism

ref   pronoun reference

P   punctuation

quot   quotation marks

rep   repetition

RD   run-on sentence

frag   sentence fragment

SS   sentence structure

sp   spelling

sp inf   split infinitive

sub   subordination

T   tense

trans   transition

⌣   transpose (change order of letters or words)

wdy   wordy

ww   wrong word

A note to the student

Contrary to many students' belief, good writing does not come naturally; even for the best writers it's mostly hard work, following the old formula of ten per cent inspiration and ninety per cent perspiration.

Writing in university or college is not fundamentally different from writing elsewhere. Yet each piece of writing has its own special purposes, and these are what determine its shape and tone. *Making Sense* will examine both the general precepts for effective writing and the special requirements of academic work (especially the essay and the report); it will also point out some of the most common errors in student composition and suggest how to avoid or correct them. Written mostly in the form of guidelines rather than strict rules—since few rules are inviolable—this book should help you escape the common pitfalls of student writing and develop confidence through an understanding of basic principles and a mastery of sound techniques.

This edition adds two new chapters: one on using illustrations, and another on writing a résumé and application letter. It also enlarges the chapter on writing an essay, providing more examples, and extends the discussion of word-processors. The intent of the original *Making Sense* remains: to give you a clear, concise, and readable guide that will help you do well on all your courses.

1

Writing and thinking

You are not likely to produce clear writing unless you have first done some clear thinking, and thinking can't be hurried. It follows that the most important step you can take is to leave yourself enough time to think.

Psychologists have shown that we don't always solve a difficult problem by "putting our mind to it" —by determined reasoning. Sometimes when we are stuck it's best to take a break, sleep on it, and let the subconscious or creative part of our brain take over for a while. Very often a period of relaxation will produce a new approach or solution. Just remember that leaving time for creative reflection isn't the same thing as sitting around listening to the stereo until inspiration strikes out of the blue.

Initial strategies

To write is to make choices. Practice makes the decisions easier to come by, but no matter how fluent you become, with each piece of writing you will still have to choose.

You can narrow the field of choice from the start if you realize that you are *not* writing for anybody, anywhere, for no particular reason. In university (or anywhere else), it's always sound strategy to ask yourself two basic questions: "What is the purpose of this piece of writing?" and "What is the reader like?" Your first reaction may be "Well, I'm writing for my teacher to satisfy a course requirement." But that's not specific enough. To be useful, your answers have to be precise.

Think about the purpose

Depending on the assignment, your purpose in writing an essay may be any one (or more) of the following:

- to show your knowledge of a topic or text;
- to show that you understand certain terms or theories;
- to show that you can do independent research;
- to show that you can apply a specific theory to new material;
- to show that you can think critically or creatively.

An assignment designed to see if you have read and understood specific material calls for a different approach from one that's meant to test your critical thinking. In the first case, your approach will tend to be *expository*, with the emphasis on presenting facts. In the second case (the main focus of the next chapter), you will probably want to structure your essay around a particular argument—an assertion that other people might dispute. Your aim in this kind of *argumentative* or persuasive essay is to bring your reader around to your point of view.

Think about the reader

Thinking about the reader does *not* mean playing up to the teacher. To convince a particular person that your own views are sound, you have to consider his or her way of thinking. If you are writing a paper on Israeli communes for a sociology professor, obviously your analysis will be different from what it would be if you were writing for an economics or history professor. You will have to make specific decisions about the terms you should explain, the background information you should supply, and the details you need to convince that particular reader. In the same way, if your reader supports the idea of universal social programs in Canada and you intend to propose programs targeting only the needy, you will have to anticipate any arguments that may be raised, in order to answer them. If you don't know who will be reading your paper—your professor, your tutorial leader, or a marker—just imagine someone intelligent, knowledgeable, and interested, skeptical enough to question your ideas but flexible enough to adopt them if your evidence is convincing.

Think about the length

Before you start writing, you will also need to think about the length of your assignment in relation to the time you have available to spend on it. If both the topic and the length are prescribed, it should be fairly easy for you to assess the level of detail required and the amount of research you need to do. If only the length is prescribed, that restriction will help you decide how broad or how narrow a topic you should choose (see p. 11-12).

Think about the tone

In everyday writing to friends you probably take a casual tone, but academic writing is usually more formal. The exact degree of formality required will depend on the kind of assignment and instruction you have been given. In some cases — say, if your psychology or philosophy professor asks you to express yourself freely and personally in a journal — you may well be able to use an informal style. Essays and reports, however, require a more formal tone. What kind of style is too informal for most academic work? Here are the main signs:

Use of slang

Although the occasional slang word or phrase may be useful for special effect, frequent use of slang is not acceptable. The reason is that slang expressions are usually regional and short-lived: they may mean different things to different groups at different times. (Just think of how widely the meanings of *hot* and *cool* can vary, depending on the circumstances.)

Excessive use of first-person pronouns

Since a formal essay is not a personal outpouring, you want to keep it from becoming *I*-centred. It's certainly acceptable to use the occasional first-person pronoun, and your reader will obviously want to know your opinions — as long as they are backed by evidence. Still, you should avoid the *I think* or *in my view* approach when the fact or argument speaks for itself. If the choice, however, is between using *I* and creating a tangle of passive constructions, it's almost always better to choose *I*. (A hint: when you do use *I*, it will be less noticeable if you place it in the middle of the sentence rather than at the beginning — a point useful for writing résumés as well as essays.) Here are some examples of ways to avoid both I-centred and unnecessarily passive sentences.

    X   Having analysed the new legislation, I believe it is flawed.

    X   The new legislation having been analysed, it appears to me to be flawed.

(better)   When analysed, the new legislation seems flawed.

    X   In this essay, Atwood's portrayal of wilderness will be investigated, and the repeated conflict between wilderness and civilization will be discussed.

(better)   In this essay, I will investigate Atwood's portrayal of nature and discuss the repeated conflict between wilderness and civilization.

(best)   This essay will investigate Atwood's portrayal of nature and discuss the repeated conflict between nature and civilization.

Frequent use of contractions

Generally speaking, contractions such as *can't* and *isn't* are not suitable for academic writing, although they may be fine for letters or other informal kinds of writing—for example, this handbook. The problem with trying to avoid excessive informality is that you may be tempted to go to the other extreme. If your writing sounds stiff or pompous, you may be using too many high-flown phrases, long words, or passive constructions (see Chapter 9).

2

Writing an essay

If you are one of the many students who dread writing an academic essay, you will find that following a few simple steps in planning and organizing will make the task easier — and the result better.

The planning stage

Some students claim they can write essays without any planning at all. On the rare occasions when they succeed, their writing is usually not as spontaneous as it seems: in fact, they have thought or talked a good deal about the subject in advance, and come to the task with some ready-made ideas. More often, trying to write a lengthy essay without planning just leads them to frustration. They get stuck in the middle and don't know how to finish, or suddenly realize that they are rambling off in all directions.

In contrast, most writers say that the planning, or pre-writing, stage is the most important part of the whole process. Certainly the evidence shows that poor planning usually leads to disorganized writing; in the majority of students' essays the single greatest improvement would not be better research or better grammar, but better organization.

This insistence on planning doesn't rule out exploratory writing (see p. 19). Many people find that the act of writing itself is the best way to generate ideas or overcome writer's block; the hard decisions about organization come after they've put something down on the page. Whether you organize before or after you begin to write, however, at some point you need to plan.

Reading primary material

Primary material is the direct evidence — usually books or articles — on which you will base your essay. Surprising as it may seem, the best way to begin working with this material is to give it a fast initial skim. Don't just start reading from cover to cover: first look at the table of contents, scan the index, and read the preface or introduction to get a sense of the author's purpose and plan. Getting an overview will allow you to focus your questions for a more purposeful and analytic second reading. Make no mistake: a superficial reading is *not* all you need. You still have to work through the material carefully a second time. But an initial skim followed by a focused second reading will give you a much more thorough understanding than one slow plod ever will.

A warning about secondary sources

Always be sure you have a firm grasp of the primary material before you turn to secondary sources (commentaries on or analyses of the primary source). Instructors in some subjects discourage secondary reading in introductory courses because they know the dangers of relying too heavily on it. If you turn to commentaries as a way around the difficulty of understanding the primary source, you may be overwhelmed by the weight of authority and produce a trite, second-hand essay. Your interpretation could even be downright wrong, since at this stage you may not know enough about a subject to be able to evaluate the commentary. Secondary sources are an important part of learning, and essential to many research papers, but they can never substitute for your own active reading of the primary material.

Analyse your subject: ask questions

Some instructors ask students to choose their own essay topics, and others simply suggest subject areas. In either case, since a subject area is bound to be too broad for an essay topic, you will have to analyse it in order to find a way of limiting it. The best way of analysing is to ask questions that will lead to useful answers.

How do you form that kind of question? Journalists approach their stories through a five-question formula: *who? what? where? when? why?* You could apply the same formula to aspects of your subject, and add *how?*

For example, starting with the question *what?* and applying it to a work of literature, you might ask, "What contrasts of character can one find?"; "What role do the minor characters play?"; "What are the good or evil qualities of the characters?" *How* and *why* questions are often the most productive, since they take you beyond information-gathering and force you to analyse and interpret. For example: "How does the author portray women?" (Or old age, or native people, and so on.)

To take another subject, consider some of the same kinds of questions about constitutional arrangements and proposals:

- *What* are the obstacles to inter-provincial free trade?

- *What* are the arguments for (or against) a triple-E senate?

- *How* are the courts affected by the Charter of Rights?

- *Why* should education and job-training be provincial responsibilities (or, alternatively, federal ones)?

Try the three-C approach

A more systematic scheme for analysing a subject is the three-C approach outlined below. It forces you to look at a subject from three different perspectives, asking basic questions about *components*, *change*, and *content*:

3-C Approach to Generating Ideas

Components:
- What are the parts of categories?
- Can the main divisions be subdivided?

Change:
- What features have changed?
- Is there a trend?
- What caused the change?
- What are the results of the change?

Context:
- What is the larger issue surrounding the subject?
- In what tradition or school of thought does the subject belong?
- How is the subject similar to, and different from, related subjects?

What are the components of the subject? In other words, how might it be broken down into smaller elements? This question forces you to take a close look at the subject and helps you avoid over-simplification or easy generalization.

Suppose that your assignment is to discuss the policies of Mackenzie King. After asking yourself about components, you might decide that you can split the subject into (1) domestic policies and (2) foreign policies. Alternatively, you might divide it into (1) economic policies,

(2) social policies, and (3) political policies. Then, since these components themselves are fairly broad, you might break them down further. Economic policies could be split into fiscal and monetary policies; social policies might be subdivided according to the different social groups targeted; political policies could be split into relations with the provinces and relations with other countries.

Similarly, if you are analysing the imagery in a Shakespearean play, you could ask, "What are the different types?" (for example, similes, metaphors, and allusions). Or, "What are the content groupings?" (for instance, animal images, solar images, or military images).

For a sociology essay on juvenile crime, you could ask, "What are the different types and frequencies of juvenile crime?" "Do crimes differ among juveniles of different sexes and ages?"

What features of the subject suggest change? This question helps you to think about trends. It can also point to antecedents or causes of an occurrence as well as the likely results or implications of a change.

Suppose you have decided to focus on Mackenzie King's economic policies. In what areas did those policies alter over a period of years? Did he express contradictory views in different documents? What caused changes in a specific policy? What were the effects of these changes?

For the essay on Shakespeare's imagery you could ask whether a pattern of repeated images emerges as the drama proceeds. Does a particular image change in its use or connotation? What is the effect of the change?

On the subject of juvenile crime you might ask, "Have there been changes or trends in the rate of criminal offences committed?" or "Have there been changes in the nature or definition of delinquency?" Then ask, "What are the causes or results of these changes?"

What is the context of this subject? Into what particular school of thought or tradition does it fit? What are the similarities and differences between this subject and related ones? The following are typical context questions:

- How do Mackenzie King's policies compare with those of other Liberal prime ministers? With Conservative policies?
- How does the use of imagery (either general or of a particular type) in play X differ from that in the earlier play Y? How does Shakespeare's use of a specific type of imagery compare with, say, Marlowe's?

- How does the rate or nature of juvenile delinquency in Canada compare with that in other countries? Or with adult criminal actions?

General as most of these questions are, you will find that they stimulate more specific questions—and thoughts—about the material, from which you can choose your topic and decide on your controlling idea. Remember that the ability to ask intelligent questions is one of the most important, though often underrated, skills that you can develop for any work, in university and elsewhere.[1]

Analysing a prescribed topic

Even if the topic of your essay is supplied by your instructor, you still need to analyse it carefully. Try underlining key words to make sure that you don't neglect anything. Distinguish the main focus from subordinate concerns. A common error in dealing with prescribed topics is to emphasize one portion while giving short shrift to another. Give each part its proper due—and make sure that you actually do what the instructions tell you to do. For example, consider the instructions implicit in these verbs:

outline   state simply, without much development of each point (unless asked).

trace   review by looking back—on stages or steps in a process, or on causes of an occurrence.

explain   show how or why something happens.

discuss   examine or analyse in an orderly way. This instruction allows you considerable freedom, as long as you take into account contrary evidence or ideas.

compare   examine differences as well as similarities (for a more detailed discussion, see pp. 21-2).

evaluate   analyse strengths and weaknesses, providing an overall assessment of worth.

These and other verbs tell you how to approach the topic; don't confuse them.

Develop a thesis

As was pointed out in Chapter 1, not all essays centre on arguments. Yet every essay, even the expository kind, needs a controlling idea around which all the material can be organized. This central idea is usually known as a thesis, though in the case of an expository essay you may prefer to think of it as a theme. Consider these statements:

THEME: Canada's ten provinces encompass a variety of cultural heritages.

THESIS: Canada could be better governed if there were fewer provinces.

The first is a straightforward statement of fact; an essay centred on such a theme would probably focus on simply describing those different heritages. By contrast, the second statement is one with which other people might well disagree; an essay based on this thesis would have to present a convincing argument. Intimidating as the argumentative form may seem, many students prefer it because it gives them a chance to stretch their intellectual muscles. It's also the easiest form to organize—and the most likely to produce strong writing.

If you have decided to present an argument, you may still have in mind a number of theses that interest you. The next step is to choose one as the focal point around which you can start organizing your material.

This "working thesis" doesn't have to be final: you are free to change it at any stage in your planning. A working thesis simply serves as a linchpin, holding together your information and ideas as you organize. It will help you define your intentions, make your research more selective, and focus your essay.

At some point in the writing process you will probably want to make your working thesis into an explicit thesis statement that can appear in your introduction. This is not always necessary: as you gain experience, you may choose to put your thesis later, or just imply rather than state it. Even if you don't intend to include it in your final draft, though, you need to know what your thesis statement is, and to keep it in mind throughout the writing process. It's worth taking the time to work this statement out carefully. Use a complete sentence to express it, and above all make sure that it is *limited, unified,* and *exact.*[2]

Make it limited

A limited thesis is one that is narrow enough to be workable. Suppose, for example, that your general subject is the Social Credit party in Canada. Such a subject is much too broad to be handled properly in an essay of one or two thousand words: you must limit it in some way and create a line of argument for which you can supply adequate supporting evidence. Following the analytic questioning process, you might find that you want to restrict it by time: "The Social Credit party in the 1970s was indistinguishable in its monetary policies from the Conservative party." Or you might prefer to limit it by geography: "The development of the Social Credit party in British Columbia had less to do with its policies than with its political opportunities."

To take an example from literature, suppose that your general subject for a two-thousand-word essay is the work of Hugh MacLennan. You might want to limit it by discussing a prominent theme in one or two novels: "Although MacLennan exposes the dark side of religion in *Each Man's Son*, he also reveals a yearning for spiritual wholeness." Or you could focus on some aspect of characterization: "In *Each Man's Son* and *The Watch That Ends the Night*, MacLennan creates drama through his contrast of character types." Whatever the discipline or subject, make sure that your topic is restricted enough that you can explore it in depth.

Make it unified

To be unified, your thesis must have one controlling idea. Beware of the double-headed thesis: "In his term as President of the United States, Lyndon Johnson introduced many social programs, but the Vietnam War issue led to his downfall." What is the controlling idea here: the success of Johnson's social programs, or the reason for his downfall? The essay should focus on one or the other. It is possible to have two or more related ideas in a thesis, but only if one of them is clearly in control, with all the other ideas subordinated to it; for example, "Despite criticism from various regions in Canada, the CBC is an instrument of national unity." Or, "Although crime rates among female juveniles are rising, the majority of young offenders are male."

Make it exact

It's important, especially in a thesis, to avoid vague terms such as *interesting* and *significant*, as in "Helmut Schmidt was Germany's most interesting Chancellor." Does *interesting* mean *effective* or *daring* in his policies, or does it mean personally *charming*? Don't say simply "Sheila Watson's use of symbols is an important feature of her writing" when you can be more precise about the work you are discussing, the kind of symbols you've found there, and exactly what they do: "In *The Double Hook*, Sheila Watson adapts traditional symbols from Christian and Indian mythology to underscore the theme of spiritual death and regeneration."

Remember to be as specific as possible in creating a thesis, in order to focus your essay. Don't just make an assertion — give the main reason for it. Instead of saying simply "Many westerners are resentful of central Canada" and leaving it at that, add an explanation: ". . . because of historic grievances, such as tariffs and freight rates, and the more recent issues of the national energy policy." If these details make your thesis stylistically cumbersome, don't worry. A working thesis is only a planning device, something to guide the organization of your ideas. The wording doesn't have to be the same in your final essay.

Research your topic

If your topic requires more facts or evidence than the primary material provides, or if you want to know other people's opinions on the subject, you will need to visit the library for research. Some students like to read around in the subject area before they decide on an essay topic; for them, the thesis comes after the exploration. You may find this approach useful for some essays, but generally it's better to narrow your scope and plan a tentative thesis before you turn to secondary sources — you'll save time and produce a more original essay.

Explore the library
The importance of getting to know your way around a library can't be stressed enough. You don't want to be so overwhelmed by its size and complexity that you either scrimp on required research or waste time and energy trying to find information. Remember that most academic libraries have orientation seminars specifically designed to show you where and how to find what you want — how to use a card or micro-fiche catalogue, for example. Take advantage of these services. Librarians will be glad to show you the bibliographies, indices, and other reference books for your field of study. Once you are familiar with these basic sources you will be able to check systematically for available material.

Computerized data bases can simplify your search for relevant sources of information, which are often scattered across a number of journals and books in different locations. A variety of data bases exist these days for most subjects, and more are likely to exist in future. Check with the librarian to see if any are available in your library for your topic and to find out exactly how to use them. A computerized search will cost you some money, depending on the number of data bases you use, but the cost is worthwhile if it eliminates many hours of manual hunting.

For any data base, you punch into the computer certain key words that describe your topic, and the computer searches for those words, or the equivalent, in *all* the titles and abstracts in the data base. It will then print out, depending on your instructions, the titles, references, and abstracts for each relevant article or book.

For example, if you want material about dyslexia among twins, you would punch in "twins" and "dyslexia" as your key words. For a broader search, you might substitute "reading" or "learning" for the narrower term "dyslexia."

If a computerized search is not available or practical, you can still conduct thorough research, by turning to bibliographies and review articles. Just remember that since printed biliographies may not be as up to date as computer data bases, you must check to make sure you have covered recent source material.

Taking good notes

Finding your research material is one thing; taking notes that are dependable and easy to use is another. With time you will develop your own best method, but for a start you might try the index-card system. Record each new idea or piece of evidence on a separate card (see below); the number you need will obviously depend on the range and type of your research. When you've finished with your note-taking, you can then easily arrange the cards in the order in which you will use them.

ARNOLD J. TOYNBEE, A Study of History
Abridgement of vols. I-IV by D.C. SOMERVELL
(New York and London: Oxford Univ. Press, 1946)

Says 20th Century follows "typical pattern of
a time of troubles: a breakdown, a rally and
a second relapse" (p. 553).

Index Card

Whatever method you follow, remember that exact records are essential for proper footnotes:

1. For every entry check that the bibliographic details are complete, including the name of the author, title, place and date of publication, and page number, as well as the library call number. Nothing is more frustrating than using a piece of information in an essay only to find that you aren't sure where it came from.

Put the main bibliographic details about the author and work on one card, and then use a separate card for each particular idea, quotation, or theory.

2. Check that quotations are copied precisely, and—since you may end up using only part of the quotation—be sure to mark any page breaks.

3. Include page numbers for every reference, even if you paraphrase or summarize the idea rather than copy it word for word.

A warning about plagiarism

Plagiarism is a form of stealing; as with other offences against the law, ignorance is no excuse. The way to avoid it is to give credit where credit is due. If you are using someone else's idea, acknowledge it, even if you have changed the wording or just summarized the main points.

There are two basic ways of giving credit:

1. *Directly* in the text: for example, "As Toynbee says, . . . " followed by a quotation, or "Toynbee makes the point that . . .", followed by a paraphrase or quotation. Direct mention makes sense when you will be referring repeatedly to the same author. Of course you still need to identify the specific source, either in a footnote or by adding the date and/or page number—e.g., (1968, 91)—in parentheses at the end of the sentence; if you choose the second method, be sure your paper includes a complete bibliography. (See Chapters 12 and 13 for more details on documentation.)

2. *Indirectly*, by mentioning only in a parenthetical reference (with a reference list at the end) or in a footnote. This method is practical when you are giving credit to more than one source—e.g., (Stolz, 1990; MacArthur, 1992)—or when a particular source will not be referred to again.

Don't be afraid that your work will seem weaker if you acknowledge the ideas of others. On the contrary, it will be all the more convincing: serious academic treatises are almost always built on the work of preceding scholars.

Where should you draw the line on acknowledgements? As a rule, you don't need to give credit for anything that's common knowledge. You wouldn't footnote lines from "O Canada," for example, or the date of Confederation or the Nazi invasion of France in the Second World War. However, you should acknowledge any clever turn of phrase that is neither well known nor your own. And always document any fact or claim—statistical or otherwise—that is unfamiliar or open to question.

Creating an outline

Individual writers differ in their need for a formal plan. Some say they never have an outline, and others maintain they can't write without one; most fall somewhere in between. Since organization is such a common problem, though, it's a good idea to know how to draw up an effective plan. Of course, the exact form it takes will depend on the pattern you use to develop your ideas—whether you are defining, classifying, or comparing, for example (see pp. 19-22).

If you have special problems with organizing material, your outline should be formal, in complete sentences. On the other hand, if your mind is naturally logical, you may find it's enough just to jot down a few words on a scrap of paper. For most students, an informal but well-organized outline in point form is the most useful model. Here is an example for an argumentative essay:

> THESIS: When Trudeau first came to power, his style was seen as an enormous asset, but by the '80s the same style was increasingly seen as a liability.

> I. Trudeau's early style perceived in positive light
>   A. Charismatic
>   1. Public adulation: "Trudeaumania"
>   2. Media awe
>   B. Intellectual
>   C. Tough
>   1. Handling of journalists
>   2. Handling of Quebec
>   D. Anti-establishment
>   1. Swinging lifestyle
>   2. Disregard for government traditions

II. Later reversal: Trudeau's image becomes negative
  A. Irritating
    1. Public opinion polls
    2. Media disenchantment
  B. Out of touch with economic reality
  C. Confrontationist
    1. With individual dissenters
    2. With Premiers
    3. With Opposition leaders
  D. Arrogant
    1. Extravagant lifestyle in time of recession
    2. Autocratic approach to governing

The following example shows an outline for an expository essay, centring on a more descriptive theme:

THEME: Because of their importance for survival, refined navigational skills are found throughout the animal kingdom. These skills are based on a wide variety of different cues.

I. Orienting and navigating seen in many different kinds of animals.
  A. Birds
    1. Arctic tern
    2. Homing pigeon
  B. Insects
    1. Army ants
    2. Monarch butterfly
  C. Fish
    1. Salmon

II. Navigating serves different purposes.
  A. Migration
    1. Favourable climate
    2. Food availability
    3. Breeding grounds
  B. Locating local food sources
    1. Honeybee

III. Navigating animals use different cues.
  A. Celestial cues
    1. Sun-compass
    2. Star navigation
  B. Terrestrial cues
    1. Geomagnetism
    2. Barometric pressure
    3. Odour trails
    4. Landmarks

The guidelines for both types of outline are simple:

Code your categories.   Use different sets of markings to establish the relative importance of your entries. The example here moves from roman numerals to letters to arabic numbers, but you could use another system.

Categorize according to importance.   Make sure that only items of equal value are put in equivalent categories. Give major points more weight than minor ones.

Check lines of connection.   Make sure that each of the main categories is directly linked to the central thesis; then see that each subcategory is directly linked to the larger category that contains it. Checking these lines of connection is the best way of preventing essay muddle.

Be consistent.   In arranging your points, be consistent. You may choose to move from the most important point to the least important, or vice versa, as long as you follow the same order every time.

Use parallel wording.   Phrasing each entry in a similar way will make it easier to be consistent in your presentation.

One final word: be prepared to change your outline at any time in the writing process. An outline is not meant to put an iron clamp on your thinking, but to relieve anxiety about where you're heading. A careful outline prevents frustration and dead ends—that "I'm stuck, where can I go from here?" feeling. But since the very act of writing will usually generate new ideas, you should be ready to modify your original plan. Just remember that any new outline must have the consistency and clear connections required for a unified essay.

The writing stage

Writing the first draft

Instead of labouring for excellence from scratch, most writers find it easier to write the first draft as quickly as possible and do extensive revisions later. However you begin, you can't expect the first draft to be the final copy. Skilled writers know that revising is a necessary part of the writing process, and that the care taken with revisions makes the difference between a mediocre essay and a good one.

Many writers face writer's block. If you are one of them, remember that you don't need to write all parts of the essay in the same order in which they are to appear in the final copy. In fact, many students find the introduction the hardest part to write. If you face the first blank page with a growing sense of paralysis, try leaving the introduction until later, and start with the first idea in your outline. If you feel so intimidated that you haven't even been able to draw up an outline, you might try John Trimble's approach and charge right ahead with any kind of beginning—even a simple "My first thoughts on this subject are . . ." .[3] Instead of sharpening pencils or running out for a snack, try to get going. Don't worry about grammar or wording; scratch out pages or throw them away if you must. Remember, the object is to get your writing juices flowing.

Of course, you can't expect this kind of exploratory writing to resemble the first draft that follows an outline. You will probably need to do a great deal more changing and reorganizing, but at least you will have the relief of seeing words on a page to work with. Many experienced writers—not only those with writer's block—consider this the most productive way to proceed.

Occasionally, people suffering from writer's block find that dictating part or all of an essay into a tape recorder overcomes the problem. This route may work for you, but it is time-consuming and can cost you money. You or someone else will have to transcribe the material into printed form before you can edit it. In any case, to avoid a wordy and rambling draft, you need to speak from a detailed plan. The more specific it is, the more coherent your first draft will be.

Developing your ideas: some common patterns

The way you develop your ideas will depend on your essay topic, and topics can vary enormously. Even so, most essays follow one or another of a handful of basic organizational patterns. Here's how to use each pattern effectively.

1. Defining

Sometimes a whole essay is an extended definition, explaining the meaning of a term that is complicated, controversial, or simply important to your field of study: for example, *nationalism* in political science, or *monetarism* in economics, or *existentialism* in philosophy.

More often, perhaps, you may want to begin a detailed discussion of a topic by defining a key term, and then shift to a different organizational pattern. In either case, make your definition exact. It should be broad enough to include all the things that belong in the category and at the same time narrow enough to exclude things that don't belong. A good definition builds a kind of verbal fence around a word, herding together all the members of the class and cutting off all outsiders.

For any discussion of a term that goes beyond a bare definition, you should, of course, give concrete illustrations or examples; depending on the nature of your essay, these could vary in length from one or two sentences to several paragraphs or even pages. If you are defining monetarism, for instance, you will probably want to discuss at some length the theories of leading monetarists.

In an extended definition, it's also useful to point out the differences between the term and any other that is connected with it or often confused with it. For instance, if you are defining *pathos* you may want to distinguish it from *tragedy*; if you are defining *common law*, you may want to distinguish it from *statute law*.

2. Classifying

Classifying means dividing something into its separate parts according to a given principle of selection. The principle or criterion may vary; you could classify crops, for example, according to how they grow (above the ground or below the ground), how long they take to mature, or what climatic conditions they require; members of a given population might be classified according to age group, occupation, income, and so on. If you are organizing your essay by a system of classification, remember the following:

- All members of a class must be accounted for. If any are left over, you need to alter some categories or add more.
- Categories can be divided into subcategories. You should consider using subcategories if there are significant differences within a category. If, for instance, you are classifying the work force according to occupation, you might want to create subcategories according to income level or sex.
- Any subcategory should contain at least two items.

3. Explaining a process

This kind of organization shows how something works or has worked, whether it be the weather cycle, the process of justice, or the stages in a political or military campaign. The important point to remember is to be systematic, to break down the process into a series of steps or stages. Although at times it will vary, most often your order will be chronological, in which case you should see that the sequence is accurate and easy to follow. Whatever the arrangement, you can generally make the process easier to follow if you start a new paragraph for each new stage.

4. Tracing causes or effects

A cause-or-effect analysis is really a particular kind of process discussion, in which certain events are shown to have led to or resulted from other events. Usually you are explaining *why* something happened. The main warning here is to avoid over-simplifying. If you are tracing causes, distinguish between a direct cause and a contributing cause, between what is a condition of the event in question and what is merely a correlation or coincidence. For example, if you find that both the age of the average driver in Canada and the number of accidents caused by drunk drivers are increasing, you cannot jump to the conclusion that older drivers are the cause of the increase in drunk-driving accidents. Similarly, be sure that anything you call a "result" of an event or action is really a consequence, rather than something that just happened to follow.

5. Comparing

One point sometimes forgotten is that comparing things means showing differences as well as similarities — even if the topic does not say "compare and contrast." Suppose, for instance that you were comparing negative and positive opinions on the effects of free trade in various sectors. The easiest method for comparison — though not always the best — is to discuss the first subject in the comparison thoroughly and then move on to the second:

> Negative views: resources
> manufacturing
> culture
> Positive views: resources
> manufacturing
> culture

The problem with this kind of comparison is that it often sounds like two separate essays slapped together. To be successful you must integrate the two subjects, first in your introduction (by putting them both in a single context) and again in your conclusion, where you should bring together the important points you have made about each. When discussing the second subject, try to refer repeatedly to your findings about the first ("unlike the critics, the supporters maintain that . . . "). This method may be the wisest choice if the subjects for comparison seem so unlike that it is hard to create similar categories by which to discuss them—if the points you are making about one are of a different type than the points you are making about the other.

If it is possible to find similar criteria or categories for discussing both subjects, however, the comparison will be more effective if you organize it like this:

resources: negative views
positive views
manufacturing: negative views
positive views
culture: negative views
positive views

Because this kind of comparison is more tightly integrated, the reader can more readily see the similarities and differences between the subjects. As a result, the essay is likely to be more forceful.

Introductions

The beginning of an essay has a dual purpose: to indicate both the topic and your approach to it, and to whet your reader's interest in what you have to say. One effective way of introducing a topic is to place it in a context—to supply a kind of backdrop that will put it in perspective. You step back a pace and discuss the area into which your topic fits, and then gradually lead into your specific field of discussion. Sheridan Baker[4] calls this the funnel approach (see p. 24). For example, suppose that your topic is the growing moral maturity of Brian O'Connal in W.O. Mitchell's *Who Has Seen the Wind?* You might begin with a more general discussion of growing up in the west, or the movement from innocence to experience in other novels. A funnel opening is applicable to almost any kind of essay. The following example is taken from an essay on the rise of complex society in Egypt:

> The great society of the Nile Valley that existed between about 3200 BC and 600 BC has aroused much public and professional interest. The spectacular pyramids and temples, however, have obscured the importance of the small predynastic villages in which Egyptian culture has its roots. The change from isolated family communities to a more complex existence with a central authority took place rapidly. In 5000 BC the Egyptians were hunters and part-time farmers, but a mere 1600 years later, they had diversified immensely. Although many general

theories exist for the rise of the Nile Valley culture, this essay will show that no single factor is responsible. Rather, many different causes, from writing, warfare, religion and agriculture to trade, social stratification and foreign influences, all played a part.[5]

It's a good idea to try to catch your reader's interest right from the start — you know from your own reading how a dull beginning can put you off. The fact that your instructor must read on anyway makes no difference. If a reader has to get through thirty or forty similar essays, it's all the more important for yours to stand out. A funnel opening isn't the only way to catch the reader's attention. Here are three of the most common leads:

The quotation. This approach works especially well when the quotation is taken from the person or work that you will be discussing. Here is an example from an essay on Virginia Woolf's *To the Lighthouse*:

> In *A Room of One's Own* Virginia Woolf sketches a "plan of the soul" for every individual, in which both male and female powers exist. "The normal and comfortable state of being," she suggests, is that "the two live in harmony together, spiritually cooperating." The main characters in *To the Lighthouse*, written two years earlier, struggle to attain this gender balance. Woolf shows that this inner harmony is constantly destroyed by the sexual attitudes of the day. She creates characters who were born androgynous, but whose natural balance is undermined by the strictures of society.

The question. The rhetorical question will only annoy the reader if it's commonplace or the answer is obvious, but a thought-provoking question can make a strong opening. For example, an essay on the issue of native people's right to self-government might begin with the question "Does native self-government mean better government?" Just be sure that you answer the question in your essay.

The anecdote or telling fact. This is the kind of concrete lead that journalists often use to grab their readers' attention. For example, a sociology paper on "latch-key" children might begin: "Jimmy sat on the front steps, bravely holding back his tears. He'd lost his key, and his mother wouldn't be home for another hour." Save this approach for your least formal essays — and remember that the incident must really highlight the ideas you are going to discuss.

Whatever your lead, it must relate to your topic: never sacrifice relevance for originality. Finally, whether your introduction is one paragraph or several, make sure that by the end of it your reader clearly knows the direction you mean to take.

Conclusions

Endings can be painful—sometimes for the reader as much as for the writer. Too often, the feeling that one ought to say something profound and memorable produces the kind of prose that suggests violins throbbing in the background. You know the sort of thing:

> Clearly the symbolism of Four Quartets is both intellectually and emotionally stimulating. Through it Eliot has produced poetry of lasting significance which will inspire readers for generations to come.

Why is this embarrassing? Because it's phony—a grab-bag of clichés.

Experienced editors often say that many articles and essays would be better without their final paragraphs: in other words, when you have finished what you want to say, the only thing to do is stop. This advice works best for short essays, where you need to keep the central point firmly in the foreground and don't need to remind the reader of it. For longer pieces, where you have developed a number of ideas or a complex line of argument, you should provide a sense of closure. Readers welcome an ending that helps to tie the idea together; they don't like to feel they've been left dangling. And since the final impression is often the most lasting, it's in your interest to finish strongly. Simply restating your thesis or summarizing what you have already said isn't forceful enough. What are the other options?

The inverse funnel. The simplest and most basic conclusion is one that restates the thesis *in different words* and then discusses its implications. Sheridan Baker calls this the inverse funnel approach, as opposed to the funnel approach of the opening paragraph.[6]

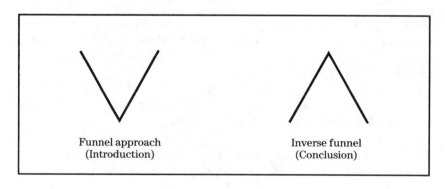

Funnel approach
(Introduction)

Inverse funnel
(Conclusion)

The same essay that provided an example of a funnel opening concludes with an inverse funnel:

> The evidence presented in this analysis suggests that writing, warfare, religion, agriculture, trade and changes in the make-up of society all contributed to the rise of complex society in Egypt. It is hard to say which cause was the most important and impossible to determine for certain the sequence of events. The most plausible theory, however, is that one factor in turn produced others. The effect is rather like that of a delicate ecosystem: one change in the environment will produce other reactions, and the greater the initial change, the greater the following ones will be. Egypt went through enormous changes during the third millenium and, as with the changes of our own century, the effect was explosive and rapid in restructuring the culture.

One danger in moving to a wider perspective is that you may try to embrace too much. When a conclusion expands too far it tends to lose focus and turn into an empty cliché, like the embarrassing first example. It's always better to discuss specific implications than to leap into the thin air of vague generalities.

Here is an ending from an essay on religious tolerance and civil duty in Locke and Rousseau—a concluding paragraph that summarizes forcefully the analysis that has preceded it:

> Jean-Jacques Rousseau's outline of the division of authority between church and state could just as easily have been written by John Locke. The two theorists have similar views about both the basic division of authority and the beneficial consequences of that division. Athough they differ in their theological references to the Old and New Testaments, they desire a similar end in the unity of the state through civil and religious contentment. The means for both is the law. For Locke the law would legislate toleration. For Rousseau it would define the moral principles common to civil duty and religious devotion. Either way, for the citizen who is truly dedicated to the salvation of his soul and the preservation of the social contract, the law would assure freedom rather than restrict it.

The new angle.   A variation of the basic inverse funnel approach is to reintroduce your argument with a new twist. Suggesting some fresh angle can add excitement to your ending. Beware of injecting an entirely new idea, though, or one that's only loosely connected to your original argument: the result could be jarring or even off-topic. Here is a short conclusion to an essay on Lawren Harris's spiritual landscapes, which turns attention to the artist's own words about them.

The main inspiration for Harris's painting was a profoundly philosophical attitude to the Canadian North, expressed within the framework of theosophical thought. It was an attitude coloured by the ideas of Wassily Kandinsky and by his own basic romanticism. Harris once said, "No man is profound enough to explain fully the nature of his own inspiration" (Harris and Colgrove, p. 7), a statement that undoubtedly reflects his understanding of the myriad of unconscious as well as conscious influences on an artist. Yet despite this reservation, Harris was more helpful than most artists in explaining what inspired and influenced those spiritual landscapes which are central to his work and his reputation.

The full circle. If your introduction is based on an anecdote, a question, or a startling fact, you can complete the circle by referring to it again in relation to some of the insights revealed in the main body of your essay.

The stylistic flourish. Some of the most successful conclusions end on a strong stylistic note. Try varying the sentence structure: if most of your sentences are long and complex, make the last one short and punchy, or vice versa. Sometimes you can dramatize your idea with a striking phrase or colourful image. When you are writing your essay, keep your eyes open and your ears tuned for fresh ways of putting things, and save the best for the end.

None of these approaches to endings is exclusive, of course. You may even find that several of them can be combined in a single essay — as in some of the preceding examples.

Integrating quotations

A quotation can benefit an essay in two ways:

- It adds depth and credibility, by showing that your position or idea has the support of an authority.
- It provides stylistic variety and interest, especially if the quotation is colourful or eloquent.

The trick is to make sure that quotations are integrated with your own discussion — that they neither dominate your ideas nor seem tacked on. To ensure that they have the desired effect, always refer to the point of a quotation: don't let it dangle on its own. Usually, the best way to do this is to make the point before the quotation:

During World War II, Mackenzie King tried to muddle through the conflict of those wanting conscription and those opposed to it by saying, "Conscription if necessary, but not necessarily conscription."

Sometimes, however, a quotation can precede the explanation—a common approach to beginning an essay, as illustrated earlier in this chapter (page 23).

If a complete sentence precedes the quotation, use a colon at the end of the introducing phrase. Otherwise use a comma:

> Margaret Thatcher stated her position firmly: "The lady's not for turning."

(or)

> Margaret Thatcher held to her position, insisting, "The lady's not for turning."

If the end of the quoted passage comes at the end of a sentence, finish with a period—unless the sentence is a question, in which case finish with a question mark *after* the quotation marks.

> Did her party believe her when she insisted that "The lady's not for turning"?

The length of a quotation can vary from a short phrase woven into the middle of sentence to a paragraph or more. Just remember that the longer the quotation, the greater the danger that it will overshadow rather than reinforce your own viewpoint: don't quote any more than you really need.

The editing stage

Often the best writer in a class is not the one who can dash off a fluent first draft, but the one who is the best editor. To edit your work well you need to see it as the reader will; you have to distinguish between what you meant to say and what is actually on the page. For this reason it's a good idea to leave some time between drafts, so that when you begin to edit you will be looking at the writing afresh rather than reviewing it from memory. Now's the time to go to a movie or play some squash—do anything that will take your mind off your work. Without this distancing period you can become so involved that it's hard to see your paper objectively.

Editing doesn't mean simply checking your work for errors in grammar or spelling. It means looking at the piece *as a whole* to see if the ideas are (1) well organized, (2) well documented, and (3) well expressed. It may mean adding some paragraphs, deleting others, and shifting still others around. It very likely means adding, deleting, and shifting sentences and phrases. Experienced writers may be able to check several aspects of their work at the same time, but if you are inexperienced or in doubt about your writing, it's best to look at the organization of the ideas before you tackle sentence structure, diction, style, and documentation.

What follows is a check-list of questions to ask yourself as you begin editing. Far from all-inclusive, it focuses on the first step: examining the organization. You probably won't want to check through your work separately for each question: you can group some together and overlook others, depending on your own strengths and weaknesses as a writer.

Preliminary editing check-list

1. Are the purpose and approach of this essay evident from the beginning?
2. Are all sections of the paper relevant to the topic?
3. Is the organization logical?
4. Are the ideas sufficiently developed? Is there enough evidence, explanation, and illustration?
5. Would an educated person who hasn't read the primary material understand everything I'm saying? Should I clarify some parts or add any explanatory material?
6. In presenting my argument, do I take into account opposing arguments or evidence?
7. Do my paragraph divisions give coherence to my ideas? Do I use them to cluster similar ideas and signal changes of idea?
8. Do any parts of the essay seem disjointed? Should I add more transitional words or logical indicators to make the sequence of ideas easier to follow?

Another approach would be to devise your own check-list based on the faults of previous assignments. This is particularly useful when you move from the overview to the close focus on sentence structure, diction, punctuation, spelling, and style. If you have a particular weak area—for example, irrelevant evidence, faulty logic, or run-on sentences—you should give it special attention. Keeping a personal check-list will save you from repeating the same old mistakes.

Nowadays, most computer word-processing packages include spell-checks that will catch typing as well as spelling errors. They are not foolproof, however, and won't point out actual words that are wrongly used (such as *there* when you need *their*), or words that are misplaced or unintentionally omitted. Think of a computer spell-check as a useful first check rather than a final one.

Similarly, computerized style checks, though considerably better than when they first appeared, are still not reliable. They will pick up common grammar errors and stylistic problems, but they do make mistakes, and will likely never equal the judgement of a good human editor.

A few words about appearance

We've all been told not to judge a book by its cover, but the very warning suggests that we have a natural tendency to do so. Readers of essays find the same thing. A well-typed, visually appealing essay creates a receptive reader and, fairly or unfairly, often gets a higher mark than a handwritten one — especially if the handwriting is messy or hard to read. Whenever possible, therefore, type your essay, and use a word-processor to do it, since it will allow you to experiment with the layout and make changes easily. On occasions when you must write by hand, as in examinations, take special care that your script is neat and easy to read, and, if your handwriting is poor, print.

Always double-space your lines and leave wide margins on sides, top, and bottom, framing the script in white. Leave three centimetres at least at the sides and top and four centimetres at the bottom, so that the reader has ample space to write comments. Number each page at the top right-hand corner, and provide a neat, well-spaced cover page that includes the title, your name, and the name of your instructor and course. Good looks won't substitute for good thinking, but they will certainly enhance it.

Tips on using a word-processor

As you may already have discovered, a computer with a relatively inexpensive, easy-to-use word-processing package can make a tremendous difference to the way you write. A word-processing system allows you to correct mistakes before they arrive on paper, rearrange your material for ease of reading, and print out a neat and tidy final copy. Most systems are easy to learn and they can speed up your writing considerably. To some extent they can also help you to improve your writing skills, because they make it easier to revise — to add, delete, or correct, to change passages, or to move paragraphs around. Here are a few simple suggestions that might be useful if you have, or are thinking of getting, a computer to do word-processing.

1. Type your material directly into the computer

The traditional way of writing a paper that eventually will be typed is to write it out in longhand, and then type it or have someone else type it for you. You can speed up the physical writing process enormously by typing your paper directly into the computer. Even if you can't type very well, you will benefit. The time spent thinking will far outweigh the time it takes to enter the words into the computer. A common argument against writing in this fashion is "I can't think at the type-writer." But once you try, you will probably find that you can. Seeing your thoughts appear in a legible form in front of you will help keep you going.

2. Try different ways of organizing your paper

Perhaps the most useful aspect of a word-processing system is that it allows you to move blocks of text around so that you can try out different ways of organizing your paper. If you have ever reached the point where your handwritten version has become so complicated that you have to write the whole thing out again in order to make any sense of it, you will appreciate being able to make on-screen corrections and rearrangements. You can set up a new organizational structure for your paper and if, after reading it through, you don't like it, you can always go back to your original version.

3. Don't let the system submerge your thinking

Seeing something typed out neatly on a screen or on paper makes it seem more acceptable than messy handwriting, even though the quality of the work may be no different. Don't be fooled into thinking that quality typing replaces quality thinking. Read over your work with a critical eye, in the knowledge that you can easily change something that is unsatisfactory. Remember that the word-processor is a tool for you to use — no more than that.

For final editing, most good writers suggest working from the printed page rather than from the computer screen. In other words, print one draft before your final copy. Your eye will get a better sense of the text by perusing a whole page at a time than by scrolling down the screen line by line.

4. Save regularly and back up your files

If you are used to working with a computer, you know the importance of this advice; if not, take it to heart. There is nothing more agonizing than to discover that something has gone wrong and caused you to lose everything you have been working on. It doesn't happen very often, but everyone experiences it at least once, and always unexpectedly. There is one easy way around the problem: when you are writing, save your work file every fifteen minutes or so. Then when your room-mate pulls the plug on the computer to turn on the TV, the most you will lose is the typing you have done since you last saved your file. A potentially more serious problem may arise if your cat decides to find out what computer disks taste like, or if you are careless with a cup of coffee. Again, a little foresight will save you from losing everything. As soon as you have completed a section of work, make a copy of it on another disk and keep it well away from the computer. An up-to-date back-up system like this will spare you a lot of frustration.

Word-processors are not the answer to all your writing needs, but if you are thinking about getting an electric typewriter, consider buying an inexpensive computer instead. It will do a lot more for you—and besides, the time spent learning the word-processing function will quickly be surpassed by the time saved in using it.

Notes

[1]For a more detailed discussion of heuristic procedures, see Richard E. Young, Alton L. Becker, and Kenneth Pike, *Rhetoric, Discovery and Change* (New York: Harcourt Brace Jovanovich, 1970), 119-36.

[2]James McCrimmon, *Writing With a Purpose*, 6th ed. (Boston: Houghton Mifflin, 1976), 18.

[3]John R. Trimble, *Writing with Style: Conversations on the Art of Writing* (Englewood Cliffs, N.J.: Prentice-Hall, 1975), 11.

[4]Sheridan Baker, *The Practical Stylist*, 5th ed. (New York: Harper and Row, 1981), 24-5.

[5]I am grateful to Dr. Margaret Proctor for providing this and other samples of essay-writing, and to Elizabeth Holliday, Kate Saunders, and other former University of Toronto students, whose essays have been adapted for this purpose.

[6]Baker, *The Practical Stylist*, 24-5.

3

Writing a book report

The term *book report* covers a variety of writing assignments, from a simple summary of a book's contents to a sophisticated literary review. In between is the kind that you will most often be asked to produce: an analytic report containing some evaluation. The following guidelines cover the three basic kinds. Before you begin your assignment, be sure to check with your instructor to find out exactly which type is expected.

The informative book report or summary

Your purpose in this kind of report is to summarize a book briefly and coherently. It's not a complicated task, but it does call on your ability to get to the heart of things, to separate what is important from what is not—a useful skill both in school and on the job. Aside from some pertinent publication information, all a simple informative report needs is an accurate summary of the book's contents.

Writing guidelines

Determine the author's purpose
An author writes a book for a reason: to cast some new light on a subject, to propose a new theory, or to bring together the existing knowledge in a field. Whatever the purpose, you have to discover it if you want to understand what guided the author's selection and arrangement of material. The best way to find out what the author intends to do is to check the table of contents, preface, and introduction.

Skim-read the book first
As noted earlier (pp. 6-7), a quick overview of the book's contents will show you what the author considers most important and what kind of

evidence he or she presents. The details will be much more under-standable once you know where the book as a whole is going.

Reread carefully and take notes

A second, more thorough reading will be the basis of your note-taking. Since you have already determined the relative importance that the author gives to various ideas, you can be selective and avoid getting bogged down in a welter of unimportant detail. Just be sure that you don't neglect any crucial passages or controversial claims.

When you are taking notes try to condense the ideas. Don't take them down word for word, and don't simply paraphrase them. You will have a much firmer grasp of the material if you resist the temptation to quote; force yourself to interpret. This approach will also help to make your report concise — remember, you want to be brief as well as clear. Condensing the material as you take notes will ensure that your report is a true summary, not just a string of quotations or paraphrases.

Pull your notes together to form a clear summary of the contents

Give the same relative emphasis to each area that the author does. Don't just list the topics in the book or the conclusions reached: discriminate between primary ideas and secondary ones.

Follow the book's order of presentation. Strictly speaking, a simple summary need not do so, but it's usually safer to follow the author's lead. That way your summary will be a clear reflection of the original.

Follow the logical chain of the arguments. Don't leave any confusing holes. You won't be able to cover every detail, of course, but you must make sure to trace all the main arguments in such a way that they make logical sense.

Include the key evidence supporting the author's argu-ments. Without some supporting details, your reader will have no way of assessing the strength of the conclusions.

Tailor the length to fit your needs. A summary can be any length, from one page to six or seven. It depends less on the length of the original material than on your purpose. If the report is an assign-ment, find out how long your instructor wants it to be. If it's for personal reference only, you will have to decide how much detail you want to have on hand.

Read and revise your report to make sure it's coherent

Summaries can often seem choppy or disconnected because so much of the original is left out. Using linking words and phrases (see p. 84) to help create a flow and give your writing a sense of logical development. Careful paragraph division will also help to frame the various sections of the summary. If the report is for a science or social science course, you can probably use headings as well to identify sections.

Include publication details

Details about the book (publisher, place and date of publication, and number of pages) must appear somewhere in your report, whether at the beginning or at the end. Follow the guidelines in Chapter 12. Separate these publication details from your discussion by a triple space.

The analytic book report

An analytic book report—sometimes called a book review—not only summarizes the main ideas in a book but at the same time evaluates them. You are best to begin with an introduction, then follow with your summary and evaluation. Publication details can come either at the beginning or at the end.

Writing guidelines

Introduction

You should provide all the background information necessary for a reader who is not familiar with the book. Here are some of the questions you might consider:

- What is the book about?
- What is the author's purpose? What kind of audience is he or she writing for? How is the topic limited? Is the central theme or argument stated or only implied?
- How does this book relate to others in its special field of interest? To other aspects of the same field?
- What are the author's background and reputation? What other books or articles has he or she written?

- Are there any special circumstances connected with the writing of this book?
- What sources has the author used?

Not all of these questions will be applicable to every book. Nevertheless, an introduction that answers some of them will put your reader in a much better position to appreciate what you have to say.

Summary

Obviously you cannot analyse a book without discussing its contents: the basic steps are the same as for the simple book summary. You may choose to present a condensed version of the book's contents as a separate section, to be followed by your evaluation; or you may prefer to integrate the two, assessing the author's arguments as you present them.

Evaluation

In evaluating the book, you might ask some of the following questions:

- How is the book organized? Are the divisions valid? Does the author give short shrift to certain areas? Is anything left out?
- What kind of assumptions does the author make in presenting the material? Are they stated or implied? Are they valid?
- Does the book accomplish what it sets out to do? Does the author's position change in the course of the book? Are there any contradictions or weak spots in the arguments? Does the author recognize those weaknesses or omissions? Remember that your job is not only to analyse the contents of the book, but to indicate its strengths and weaknesses.
- What kind of evidence is presented to support the author's ideas? Is it reliable and up to date? Are any of the data distorted or misinterpreted? Could the same evidence be used to support a different case? Does the book leave out any important evidence that might weaken its case? Is the author's position convincing?
- Does the author agree or disagree with other writers who have dealt with the same material or problem? In what respect?
- Is the book clearly written and interesting to read? Is the writing repetitious? Too detailed? Not detailed enough? Is the style clear? Or is it plodding, or jargonish, or flippant?
- Does the book raise issues that need further exploration? Does it present any challenges or leave unfinished business for the author or other scholars to pick up?
- To what extent would you recommend this book? What effect has it had on you?

The literary review

The literary review is a variation of the analytic book report. Although literature is its most frequent subject, it may deal with a wide range of topics, from art and music to the social sciences. The term "literary" refers to the presentation rather than to the material discussed: the review should stand on its own merit as an attractive piece of writing.

The advantage of a literary review is the freedom it allows you in both content and presentation. You may emphasize any aspect you like, as long as you leave your reader with a basic understanding of what the book is about. In most cases, your purpose is simply to provide a graceful introduction to the work based on personal assessment of its most intriguing — or annoying — features. Just don't be too personal: some reviewers end up telling us more about themselves than about the book. Although a literary review is usually less comprehensive than an analytic report, it should always be thoughtful, and your judgement must never be superficial.

The best way of learning how to write good literary reviews is to read some of them. Check the book review sections of a magazine such as *Saturday Night* or the weekend edition of *The Globe and Mail* to see different approaches. Pay particular attention to the various techniques that reviewers use to catch the reader's interest and hold it. The basic rule is to reinforce your comments with specific details from the book; concrete examples will add authenticity and life to your review.

Chapter

4

Writing a lab report

Students in the sciences and social sciences are often asked to report formally on the results of scientific experiments. Although lab reports generally conform to a basic format, each discipline (chemistry, physics, biology, psychology, etc.) has slightly different requirements.

Any kind of academic writing should be clear, concise, and forceful, but for scientific writing there is one more imperative: be objective. Scientists are interested in exact information, in the orderly presentation of factual evidence to support theories or claims. You must never allow your preconceived opinions or biases, or even expectations, to get in the way of the facts or distort them. You must present your information in such a way that anyone who reads your report or attempts to duplicate your procedure would be likely to reach the same conclusions that you did.

Purpose and reader

As an undergraduate, you will most often write lab reports to demonstrate that you understand a theory or process, or that you know how to test a certain hypothesis. Since your reader is your instructor, you can assume that he or she will be familiar with scientific terms; therefore you do not need to define or explain them. You can also assume that your reader will be on the look-out for any weaknesses in methodology or analysis and any omissions of important data. Usually you will be expected to give details of your calculations, but even when all you have been asked to give is the results of your calculations, you should include any experimental uncertainty that might affect them.

Format

Since the information in scientific reports must be easy for the reader to find and assess, it should be grouped into separate sections, each with a heading. One of the differences between writing lab reports and writing essays is that in a report you should use headings and subheadings whenever possible, as well as graphs, tables, or diagrams (see Chapter 6). Most lab reports follow a standard order:

1. Title page
2. Abstract or summary
3. Introduction
4. Materials

5. Method
6. Results
7. Discussion
8. Conclusion

Depending on the amount of information you have in each area, you may choose to combine certain sections.

Title page

The first page of the report is your title page. It should include the title of the experiment, the date it was performed, your name, and the date of submission; for practical purposes it should also include the name of your course and instructor. Your title should be brief but informative, clearly indicating the subject and scope of your experiment. Avoid meaningless phrases, such as "A study of . . ." or "Observations on . . ."; simply state *what* it is that you are studying, such as "The effects of background music on the concentration span of hyperactive children."

Abstract

Also known as a summary, the abstract appears on a separate page following the title page. It is a brief summary of the purpose of the experiment, as well as the method, results, and conclusion. For a simple experiment your abstract may only be a few lines; even for a complex one, you should keep it to about two hundred words.

Introduction

The introduction gives a more detailed statement of purpose or objective. If, as is often the case, your purpose is to test a hypothesis arising from a specific problem, you should clearly and explicitly state the nature of both the problem and the hypothesis. Your introduction should include the theory underlying the experiment and any pertinent background data or equations. Although you may refer to papers relevant to the experiment, it's best to avoid quoting extensively.

Materials

This section should provide a list of the materials and equipment used and some explanation of how the experiment is set up. If different arrangements of equipment are required, give a full list of the equipment in this section, and then in the *Method* section describe each separate arrangement before you describe the respective tests. When the description of the materials is short, you may combine this section with the *Method* section. Many departments encourage students in first- and second-year courses to have a single *Materials and Methods* section.

A simple diagram will help the reader to visualize the arrangement of equipment. If the diagram is too large to fit a regular page, you can draw it on an appropriately labelled attachment at the back of the report, and refer to it within the body of the report.

Note that some departments require that you specify the source or supplier of any reagents you have used. Such information should be included in this section: for example, "Spectroscopic grade carbon tetrachloride (99% pure) was obtained from B.D.H. Chemicals."

Method

This section is a step-by-step description of the procedures in the order in which you actually performed them. It must be written with enough detail that others will have no difficulty in repeating the experiment. If you are following instructions in a lab manual, you may not need to copy them out word for word; simply refer to the instructions and give details of any deviation. When a certain procedure is long, complicated, or not necessary to a full understanding of the experiment, you may describe it in a labelled attachment at the end of the report.

If you have undertaken a number of tests, you should begin with a short summary statement listing and numbering the tests so that the reader will be prepared for the series. To avoid confusion you should describe the tests in the same order in which you have listed them, giving them the same numbers and subheadings.

Although you should be concise in your description of the experimental method, make sure that you don't omit essential details. If you heated a test tube, for example, you must report at what temperature it was heated and for how long. If you performed a chromatography or other process at a faster or slower rate than usual, you must state the rate. Readers must know exactly what controls to apply if they try to perform the experiment themselves.

You should describe your experiments in the past tense. When you want to give instructions rather than a description of your method, use the imperative: for example, "Cut off 1 cm from the bottom of the stem."

Scientists writing for scientific journals are divided as to whether you should use the active or passive voice. Many prefer to use the passive voice ("The beaker was heated," rather than "I heated the beaker") because they believe that its impersonal quality helps to maintain the detached, clinical tone appropriate to a scientific report. Nevertheless, many scientists now use the active voice ("I heated the beaker") because it is clearer and less likely to lead to awkward, convoluted sentences. Ask your instructor about the department's preferences. Whichever voice you use, remember to strive for both clarity and objectivity.

Results

This is the section of most interest to scientists, and they depend on its accuracy. It usually contains a mix of data and verbal description. It will also likely contain some statistical calculations.

Find out from your instructor whether you are expected to give the details of your calculations or only the results of those calculations. In either case, you should pay special attention to the units of any quantities: to omit or misuse them is a serious scientific mistake. Taking care to include all units will also reveal mistakes in your calculations that might otherwise go undetected. If your units don't cancel properly to yield the result you expect, you will know that you have made an error.

You should also make sure where possible that the calculated values you report include the "uncertainty" in each of them. For example, you might report that the calculated volume of a hollow sphere is $23.45 \pm .05$ cc (where $\pm .05$ is the uncertainty in the volume measurement). When reporting any calculations or measurements, check to see if you need to include the standard deviation, the standard error of the mean, or the coefficient of variation.

The format of the *Results* section depends on the type of experiment performed. Generally it begins with the main finding and then deals with secondary ones. Whenever possible, summarize your results in a graph or table. A graph or chart (whether bar chart or pie chart) is usually preferable to a table, since it has more visual impact. However, if you have made several measurements you are probably best to report in tabular form. Whatever type of figure or table you use, label it clearly and be sure to refer to it and explain it in the text.

Computer programs can help you create a variety of graphs and charts. If you are working by hand, though, be sure to use properly ruled graph paper and black ink. In addition, with or without a computer, remember these guidelines:

- use a scale that will allow you to distribute your data points as widely as possible on the page;
- put the independent variable (the one you have manipulated) on the horizontal axis, and the dependent variable (the one you measure) on the vertical axis;
- make the vertical axis about three-quarters the length of the horizontal axis;
- put error bars (±) on data points, where possible;
- label the axes, including the units used, or use a legend on the side, so that the reader knows exactly what you have plotted on the graph;
- title the graph and label it (for example, "Figure 1"), so that you can refer to it by number in your report.

Discussion

This part of the lab report allows you the greatest freedom, since in it your purpose is to examine and interpret the test results and to comment on their significance. You want to show how the test produced its outcome, whether expected or unexpected, and to discuss those elements that influenced the results. In determining what details to include in the analysis section, you might try to answer the following questions:

- Do the results reflect the objective of the experiment?
- Did the experimental method help you to accomplish the purpose of the test?
- Do the results obtained agree with previous results as reported in the literature on the subject? If not, how can you account for the discrepancy between accepted values and those you have found

experimentally? What (if anything) probably went wrong during your experiment, and why? What was the source of any error?
• Can the results have another explanation?

For a good discussion, remember to think critically not only about your own work, but about how it relates to previous work.

Conclusion

This is a simple statement of the experiment's conclusion. You don't necessarily need a separate section; the conclusion can also appear as a short summary at the end of the *Discussion* section. You may include a table if you think that a graphic presentation will clarify the conclusion.

References

You should list the sources of any information used in your report. If you need to acknowledge a number of sources, you may list them in separate categories, such as *Books* and *Journals*. For details on the correct form for scientific documentation, see Chapter 13.

Report-writing style

Scientific reports, like essays, must be written with the reader in mind. Since your reader is your instructor, you don't need to define elementary terms or explain a method that would be taken for granted by anyone with scientific training. At the same time, you should avoid filling your report with technical jargon when non-technical language will suit just as well. The watchwords are clarity and precision; you want to make it easy for the reader to understand exactly what you mean.

Although the basic rules are the same as for any other kind of writing, scientific reports do pose special problems for students. Here are a few words of advice:

Avoid using too many nouns as adjectives
Clusters of nouns used as adjectives can create cumbersome phrases:

orig. Adult male kidney disease
rev. Kidney disease in adult males

orig. Apparatus construction
rev. Construction of apparatus

Of course, some nouns are frequently and quite acceptably used as adjectives: for example, *kidney* disease, *hydrogen* bomb, *reaction* time, *S.I.* units. Your ear is probably the best judge of what is awkward and what is not.

Avoid using too many abstract nouns
Whenever possible, choose a verb rather than an abstract noun:

orig. The <u>addition</u> of acid and subsequent <u>agitation</u> of the solution resulted in the <u>formation</u> of crystals.

rev. When acid <u>was added</u> and the solution <u>shaken</u>, crystals <u>formed</u>.

rev. When I <u>added</u> acid to the solution and <u>shook</u> it, crystals <u>formed</u>.

Avoid vague qualifiers
As a scientist you must be exact. In particular, you should avoid words such as *quite, very, fairly, some,* or *many,* when you can use a more exact term. *Relatively* is especially dangerous unless you are actually relating two or more things.

Avoid unnecessary passive constructions
Although you may prefer to use passive verbs for describing methods and results, you should try to use active verbs in your *Introduction, Discussion,* and *Conclusion* sections. Your sentences will be clearer and more direct:

orig. pH4 <u>is needed</u> for the enzyme.
rev. The enzyme <u>needs</u> pH4.

orig. It <u>was reported</u> by E.A. Robinson . . .
rev. E.A. Robinson <u>reported</u> . . .

Avoid ambiguous pronouns
A pronoun will cause confusion if the reader can't tell which noun it refers to:

orig. To germinate, the seed required water. <u>It</u> must be warm.

Is it the seed or the water that must be warm? If there is any chance of ambiguity, you should repeat the noun:

rev. The <u>water</u> must be warm.

(or)

rev.   The <u>seed</u> must be warm.

Be especially careful that the demonstrative pronoun *this* clearly refers to a specific noun:

orig.   When removed from the water, the stalk lost its leaves. <u>This</u> occurred over eight hours.

rev.   When removed from the water, the stalk lost its leaves. <u>This loss</u> occurred over eight hours.

5

Writing a business report

In many business courses you will have to write the kind of formal report used in the business world. This chapter shows you how to do it. Details will depend on the circumstances, but these guidelines will give you the general strategies and techniques for effective report-writing, whether in school or on the job. Remember that course reports are usually hypothetical exercises designed to see if you understand the process of writing an actual report.

Planning the report

First principles

Business managers with many demands on their time want to know the central idea of a report as quickly as possible. They also want to trust in its accuracy. When writing a business report, therefore, try to follow three basic principles:

1. Put the most important information up front, unless you have a particular reason to do otherwise. In fact, in most cases it's a good idea to put the essence of what you want to say in your first page or so — just in case that's all a busy reader happens to read.

2. Be concise. A report should say as much as possible in as little space as possible.

3. Be objective. Readers must be confident that the information you are providing is free of personal biases. Logical analysis will make your work believable (for more details, see p. 54).

Defining the task: the four R's

A business report that is off-target or of little interest to the reader is more likely to be filed than acted on. To create a focused and interesting report, you need to plan carefully. As in any other kind of writing, the time you spend organizing your thoughts and devising your strategies is well worth the effort. The first step is to define precisely what it is that you have to do. Before you even begin to write, examine the task by asking questions about four aspects: Reason, Reader, Restrictions, and Research. (Don't forget that for course work you still have to define the task as if it were the real thing.)

1. What is the reason?

Why are you writing this report? What goal is it supposed to achieve? Broadly speaking, every report has one of two basic purposes: either to provide information, or to recommend some course of action. Many informational reports such as progress, production, or monthly sales reports are used regularly to pass along facts as they accumulate; unless they focus on exceptional rather than routine matters, such reports tend to be treated as a kind of bureaucratic busy work. On the other hand, reports that are written to fill specific needs—to help someone make a decision, or to suggest a solution to a particular problem—usually receive close attention from both writer and reader. Examples would be suggestions for a new product line, a feasibility study on a proposed plant location, or recommendations for reversing a sales decline. Fortunately, this is the kind of challenging report you will be asked to write for most courses. It provides the most opportunity for you as the writer to show your ability to make inferences and judgements—both marks of managerial competence.

Determining the reason for such a report means establishing both its purpose and its expected outcome. If an important decision rests on your report, you will have to consider exactly what information is needed to make that decision, and precisely how you will support any recommendations.

2. Who is the reader?

Although a non-routine report may be read by several people, it is usually directed to one primary reader. Identifying your reader will enable you to organize and present your material in such a way that it's likely to be well received. (Your instructors will analyse your work from the relevant business perspective.) Among the details you should consider are these:

What type of person is the reader? Often the reaction will depend less on the nature of the reader's job than on his or her personality. A cautious, conservative person might favour a carefully understated position, whereas a bold, creative type might prefer a more daring approach. If your personal knowledge of the reader is slight, you can probably find someone reliable to give you a few clues.

What is the relationship? Is the reader your boss, or a colleague? How has he or she reacted to past communications with you? If you are writing for someone in a position far up the line from you, your tone and approach will probably be more formal than they would be for an associate you talk to often.

Has the reader asked for the report? If you are writing in response to a request, you may not need to fill in much detail about the purpose, but if the report is unsolicited you should take care to place it in a context.

What is the reader's field of interest or responsibility? You will need to go into more detail about an area that is your reader's specialty than you will for one in which he or she is less interested. Usually top management will want an overview, whereas a specialist will require all the particulars.

In the business world your report might be going to several different kinds of readers—to a plant supervisor, say, as well as to top management. If so, you could consider giving the complete analysis to the supervisor, and sending top management only an executive summary.

How is the reader likely to respond to the report? Consider the reader's situation and the expectations and concerns that he or she is likely to have. If you can anticipate probable objections or concerns and answer them in the report itself, your work will be that much more convincing.

How might the reader benefit from the report? Your suggestions will be more persuasive if you can point out their advantages for the reader. The benefit could be significant: giving the reader a competitive edge in the marketplace, for example, or saving the business itself from impending financial collapse. Even if the benefit is a more general one, such as improving the reader's ability to anticipate future problems, you should point it out.

3. What are the restrictions?

From the outset, you will have to consider the practical restrictions on your writing. How much time do you have? How much help is available for typing the report and for producing illustrations, photographs, or models?

Other kinds of restriction will apply to the subject of the report. Since it's always better to do a thorough job on a narrow subject than a superficial job on a broad one, you must limit your topic to manageable proportions. If you are doing a report on newspaper readership, for example, you could consider restricting it by time (a specific year or years), by geography (a certain region or market), or by kind (daily or weekly papers).

At the same time you should take into account the reader's time restrictions. For instance, it would be an annoying waste of his or her time to include in a marketing plan for a small business an option for television advertising that is too expensive to consider seriously. Careful focusing of the topic will spare your reader the trouble of going through unnecessary material.

4. What research is required?

In deciding what information to gather, you should weigh the time and money required to do the research against its usefulness to the report. In other words, you must determine what is essential.

Research decisions will be easier if you work out your topic in precise terms. A topic such as "A Report on Computers" is too vague to be useful; it will be much more helpful if you can be specific: "A Cost-Benefit Analysis of Three Micro-Computers for Use in the Accounting Department of Dominion Appliances." You should then consider research needs in relation to the first three R's: Reason, Reader, and Restrictions.

It's especially useful to determine how much your readers already know; many will need no background information at all. If you must provide some, remember that too much detail will draw attention away from more important matters. (One solution would be to attach a short background section as an appendix at the end of the report.)

Once you have decided on the information you need, you should ask yourself what, if anything, you have to verify. Is your source reliable? Should you cross-check any facts or figures? Remember that a source with a special interest in the matter may either exaggerate or gloss over certain aspects. Statistics themselves may not lie, but they can easily distort the picture.

Finally, you should determine the degree of accuracy or precision required for any figures you supply. Indicating the margin of error will show the reader that you are thorough and objective.

Often the facts and figures you need can be obtained internally, either by questioning people on the job or by researching company documents. If you find that an earlier report covers some of the same ground you are working on, you could well refer to it and make use of what you need, up-dating as necessary. If wider research is required, you will find librarians helpful in locating relevant government documents, company reports, or academic studies. (Of course, when you use another person's material you must acknowledge it and give proper references: see Chapter 12.)

When you have to obtain your own data — through a questionnaire or survey, for example — make sure that any statistical results are based on an appropriate sample. If you aren't familiar with proper sampling methods yourself, consult someone who is: nothing will weaken your credibility more than providing unreliable or invalid statistical information. Research information is only as valuable as it is accurate.

Organizing your information

The next step is to decide on the most effective way of organizing the information you have gathered. The order will depend on both the nature of the report and the anticipated response of the reader to any recommendations you make. You can follow either of two basic approaches:

1. The direct (deductive) approach
This is the most common order nowadays. Use it if your report is the routine informational kind or if you expect the reader to respond favourably or with interest to your recommendations or conclusions. The most important information (usually the recommendations or conclusions) comes before the supporting material:

1. Purpose   3. Method
2. Recommendations (Conclusions)   4. Findings

Report writers sometimes resist this order because it puts the conclusions before the analysis that led to them. However, major consulting firms and others who routinely use the direct approach have discovered that it appeals to most readers. Since your instructor may be one of the exceptions, check first to discover his or her preference.

2. The indirect (inductive) approach

This approach may be a good choice if you think that your reader's initial response to your conclusions or recommendations will be unfavourable. Instead of emphasizing your conclusions right away, you lead into them gradually, showing in a careful, step-by-step way how you reached them. If your logic and research are sound, the reader should find your conclusions inevitable. Here is the basic order:

1. Purpose
2. Method
3. Findings
4. Recommendations (Conclusions)

Often a long formal report will follow this order, but in effect change the format to a direct one by beginning with a summary that condenses the recommendations or conclusions:

1. Summary of Recommendations (Conclusions)
2. Purpose
3. Method
4. Findings
5. Details of Recommendations (Conclusions)

Many organizations insist on an added Executive Summary on a separate page at the front of any report—even if the order is direct (giving the recommendations at the beginning.) Although not always required for an academic course, it is good practice in business, since this is often the only part of a report that a busy executive will read. The Executive Summary is a stand-alone piece, aimed at the reader who wants a general overview of the important points. The report itself repeats the summary in more detail.

You will find it easier to write the Executive Summary last, after you have completed the report, even though you put it at the front, directly after the cover page.

Organizing the details

The principle of "important things first" also applies to the arrangement of points within each section. In the *Recommendations* section especially, it's a good idea to put your most important point at the beginning and give the rest in descending order of importance. If you are trying to persuade a hostile or skeptical reader, however, you might be wise to begin with the point, major or minor, that will get the most favourable reaction.

The *Findings* section, usually the most detailed part of a report, may require a different approach, especially if it is long. When you have a lot of material to cover, you should try to let your purpose determine the way you arrange it. For instance:

- to present a benefits plan, you could *divide* or *classify* the information according to the different types of employee or the different parts of the plan:
- to describe a process, you could present the stages in *chronological* order;
- to discuss differing markets for a product, you could follow a *spatial* order, arranging your findings according to geographical regions.

At other times, you may simply want to follow the order of importance used in your listing of recommendations.

Ordering for comparison

When you are presenting information from which a choice will be made, you should order it in such a way that the reader will be able to compare the options easily. For example, suppose that you have been asked to suggest a micro-computer for an office and are considering three models: Computer X, Computer Y, and Computer Z. Comparisons will be easier for your reader to make if, instead of presenting the strengths and weaknesses of each model in turn, you first decide on the criteria for comparison, and then for each criterion compare all three models. With four criteria—memory capacity, software, cost, and expandability—the plan for your *Findings* section might look like this:

A. Computer X has the best memory capacity.
   1. Computer X
   2. Computer Y
   3. Computer Z

B. Computer X has the widest range of software.
   1. Computer X
   2. Computer Y
   3. Computer Z

C. Computer Z is the least expensive.
   1. Computer X
   2. Computer Y
   3. Computer Z

D. Computer X is the most expandable.
1. Computer X
2. Computer Y
3. Computer Z

Whichever way you choose to order the details, remember to be systematic and consistent. In addition, it's a good idea to include a chart, table, or matrix to illustrate visually the points of comparison (see Chapter 6).

Beginnings

An internal office report may require nothing more than a memo heading. For more formal reports, however, you will have to supply some or all of the following:

Title page. The title you choose should be as precise and descriptive as possible: not just "Feasibility Study: Plant Location," for example, but "A Comparison of Possible Central Ontario Locations for the Monarch Auto Parts Plant." The title page should also indicate who requested the report, who wrote it, and the date of presentation:

Prepared for Arthur Jones, President
Monarch Industries Ltd.
by
Michelle Smart
Ace Consultants
June 10, 1993

(For a course assignment, don't forget to include the necessary academic information, such as course name or number.)

Table of contents. A table of contents is helpful in a long report because it allows the reader to find specific information quickly. Formats may vary. To be clear, however, you should number the sections according to their numbering in the report, and indent subheadings. Place page numbers in a corresponding column at the right-hand side of the page.

Letter of transmittal. This is a personal letter or memo to the intended reader, common in business writing but usually not required for student assignments. Most often attached to the front of the report, it may also be placed after the title page, before the Executive Summary.

The letter usually opens with a sentence about the context of the report, then moves to a brief outline of its main features. It then may acknowledge the help of others in preparing the report. Usually it closes with a goodwill statement looking to the future. Here is an illustration:

> Last summer you asked the Student Affairs Committee to investigate Campus Security. Here is the report on our investigation.
>
> Our main recommendation is that the Student Council, with the cooperation of the Student Volunteer Bureau, establish an evening escort service to safeguard students walking across isolated areas of the campus at night. This service would benefit not only part-time and extension students going home from classes, but also students who need to work late in the library or computer rooms.
>
> In conducting our investigation, we were grateful for the support of your administrative assistant, Felicia Penofsky. Her suggestions made the task much easier.
>
> When you have had the time to read and think about our recommendations, we would welcome the chance to discuss them with you.

Sometimes the letter of tranmsittal provides a complete summary of the report, replacing the Executive Summary.

Endings

After the main body of your report, you may include one or both of the following:

Appendix. An appendix contains any material that provides a useful backup but is not essential to the report. It might include added tables; the questionnaire used in a survey; summaries of raw data; parts of other reports that are pertinent to your findings; or any other information that would slow the reader down unnecessarily if it appeared in the main text.

Bibliography. This should include any documents, published or unpublished, used in preparing the report. Items should be listed in alphabetical order. You have format options, as outlined in the discussion of documentation in Chapter 12, but it's usually wisest to follow the conventions of your organization. If you have made specific references to outside sources, you should also provide footnotes or parenthetical citations, but these are rare in business reports.

Writing the report

Like any other kind of writing, writing for business should be clear, concise, and forceful (see Chapter 9). Here are some additional guidelines that are especially useful for business reports:

1. Be objective

A business report must be as free as possible of biases and subjective opinions. Your reader will be more likely to accept your findings if you follow these suggestions:

Identify your assumptions. If you are comparing microcomputers, for example, and you assume that portability is not a factor, you should say so.

Avoid unsubstantiated judgements. Be sure that any suggestions you make or conclusions you reach follow from the information you have given. Never imply anything that you cannot prove. If your findings aren't foolproof, show where the uncertainty lies.

Avoid subjective language. Words such as *terrible* or *fantastic* detract from the objective tone you want. Instead of saying "sales have shown an amazing increase," give the exact percentage of the increase and let the facts speak for themselves.

The overall tone to aim for depends on the circumstances — particularly the intended reader. If you are writing a short informal report to someone you often see, familiar terms such as *I* or *you* are appropriate, but many formal reports try to avoid the subjective impression created by personal pronouns. The result, unfortunately, is often a cumbersome load of passive constructions (see pp. 87-8). If you are writing for a group or organization, you can use the pronoun *we*, which seems less intrusive. If you are writing as an independent person, however, you don't have that option. Instead, try to recast the sentence, keeping an active verb while avoiding *I*:

   ✗   The purchasing system has been found to increase the duplication of forms.

   ✗   I found that the purchasing system increases the duplication of forms.

   ✓   The purchasing system increases the duplication of forms.

If you can't revise this way, you are better to use the odd *I* than to strangle your meaning in a convoluted *I*-less sentence. In any case, don't substitute *the writer* or *the researcher* for *I*.

2. Be specific

Although you don't have to give complete descriptive details for every fact you report, you should be as precise as possible when referring to people, places, times, and amounts — especially if you think the information might be disputed. Instead of saying

> Some time last month the president contacted the plant management and learned that some of the machines were not in operation

say

> On May 25, Arthur Smith spoke to Len Jones, the plant manager, and learned that two of the punching machines had broken down.

Take care also to be specific in defining key terms. Precision is particularly important in the case of words such as *reliable*, which may have a special technical meaning to some people but a more general one to others. To avoid confusion you must make sure that your readers know exactly how you are using such terms.

Finally, remember that by being specific, you will make your writing not only more clear but more interesting as well: concrete language is lively language. (For more details, see pp. 88-9.)

3. Use headings to tell the story

A report, unlike an essay, should use headings to distinguish the various sections. You may use a heading simply to indicate the topic of each section — for example, *Findings* — but it will be much more effective if it or a subheading summarizes the most important point. Headings that "tell the story" enable the reader to find the key points in your report at a glance. For example, *Reduced Inventories* or *Inconsistent Lay-off Policies* tells more than *Inventories* or *Lay-offs*. The outline for the micro-computer report (p. 51) provides a fuller illustration.

4. Number each section

Numbering helps to indicate each section's relative importance. Here are the three basic systems:

Roman numeral	Alphanumeric	Decimal
I.	A.	1.0
A.	1.	1.1
1.	a.	1.11
2.	b.	1.12
B.	2.	1.2
II.	B.	2.0

Most technical reports use the decimal system. Whichever method you choose, be sure to use equivalent symbols for sections of equivalent importance.

5. List information
Whenever you can simplify your material by listing it, do so. A list, like a heading, is an aid to quick understanding. As a guideline, list any sequence of three items or more. If you will be referring to the items in the list later, number each one; otherwise you may simply use a dash (—) or a bullet (•).

6. Create visual appeal
Tables, charts, and other illustrations are common and useful in reports, especially those that analyse a quantity of data. Such visual aids can help the reader grasp quickly what would take many words to explain. Use visual aids wherever you can to summarize or pull together information—but not simply to repeat what you have said in words. See Chapter 6 for guidelines on creating effective illustrations.

When using any of these visual aids, you must decide on the importance of the information it contains. If the information is supplementary, place it in an appendix. If it's essential, try to position the illustration next to the relevant discussion in the text. If you must place it at the end of the text, make sure that you number and label it, and that in the text you refer both to the illustration itself and to the point it makes: for example, "As Exhibit 2 shows, costs have decreased for each of the last five years."

Here are some other suggestions for producing a report that is appealing to the eye as well as the mind:

• Leave a generous amount use of space around the typescript to create a pleasing impression; wide margins and spaces between sections will help to break up an imposing mass of type.
• Make headings stand out by underlining them or using boldface.
• According to the relative importance of each heading and sub-heading,
  —vary the typeface. Upper-case letters (capitals) indicate more importance than lower-case letters do.
  —change the position of the headings.

Systems for the position and typeface of headings vary, but this is a common one:

PRIMARY HEADING CENTRED AND IN CAPITALS

Secondary Heading at Left Margin

The heading is underlined. The initial letter of the first and other important words are in capitals, and the text begins on a new line below.

Third-level heading. The heading is also underlined and often indented at the margin, but only the first letter of the first word is in capitals. The text follows on the same line.

With word-processors, you can make headings stand out even more by putting them in boldface type. You can also readily change the size and style of the lettering. Just remember that too many variations in type style can create a cluttered look. The watchwords for headings with visual appeal are clarity and consistency.

6

Using illustrations

Nowadays, most people are accustomed to seeing and interpreting visual representations of ideas. From international traffic symbols to "dangerous substance" signs to business logos, visual symbols and illustrations are becoming part of our everyday lives. This increased reliance on the visual may result in part from the influence of television. It also reflects the multicultural nature of our society and the increasing need to communicate quickly with a variety of language groups. Whatever the diverse reasons, graphics have impact. The pictorial representation of information or a concept can indeed be worth a thousand words: it allows us to *see* the point.

Especially when writing reports, consider whether you could display some of your information visually rather than solely through verbal discussion. It does not take much drawing skill to present a good visual. Graph paper will help. Even more helpful are the computer software programs for graphics. Whichever method you choose, remember these tips:

- Information in an illustration should expand on or complement information in the text — not simply duplicate it.
- Simple illustrations are better than cluttered ones. The easier it is for the reader to grasp the information quickly and accurately, the better the visual aid.
- Give an explanatory title for each illustration, unless it flows immediately from the preceding text — in which case a title is optional. As in report headings and subheadings, try to make the title reflect the point of the illustration, not just the topic. When this is not possible, at least be specific about the content. For example, *April Decline in Employment* or *Ontario Job Market: Monthly Employment Figures* is better than a simple *Sales Figures*.

- Label each part of the illustration clearly. If there is not room within the illustration, create a legend or key to the illustration at the side, identifying each part.
- Refer to every illustration in the text, mentioning why it is there — or what it explains. If you have several illustrations, number each (for example, *Exhibit 1*), so that you can refer to it by number in the discussion:

> . . . (See Exhibit 1.)
> As Exhibit 1 shows, . . .

Instead of labelling every illustration an "exhibit," some writers like to distinguish between tables and figures (charts, graphs, and so on). Find out what the preferred practice is in your subject area.

Kinds of visual aids

Visual aids come in many forms. The most common in scientific and business writing are tables and charts (including graphs), which can pull together quantitative data; however, for qualitative information, a matrix may be the most useful choice. Here are some guidelines for when and how to use each of these:

A table is useful when the reader needs to know many precise figures: for example, the exact prices of certain items for each year in a five-year period. It is the sensible choice for data too detailed to be

Table

First Quarter Corporate Profits, 1991

Company	$ millions	Percentage change from 1990
Xenon Corp.	$5.6	+ 13%
Mayfair Industries	8.3	+ 10.2%
Dominion Consolidated	4.5	+ 1%
C.R.C. Ltd.	7.2	− 1%

worked into a simple chart. An example might be a cost breakdown of several advertising campaigns or the sales figures for a number of products in different regions. If a table is placed right after the section of the text that describes it, the title can be omitted.

When in doubt about the amount of detail to include, remember that too much data can make a table difficult to understand. It may be better to create two tables than to clutter a single one with an overdose of information.

Charts come in three basic kinds, each suited to a particular purpose. They can dramatize information more effectively than tables and are easier for the reader to grasp. Whenever practical, therefore, try to make use of these graphic illustrations:

The line chart or graph shows change over a period of time; it's often used to point out trends or fluctuations in trends, as in a sales report. In devising a graph, be sure to use a scale that will distribute the data points over the total space. Put quantities on the vertical axis and time values on the horizontal axis. Try to shape the dimensions of the graph to give an accurate visual impression of the extent of change.

Line Chart or Graph

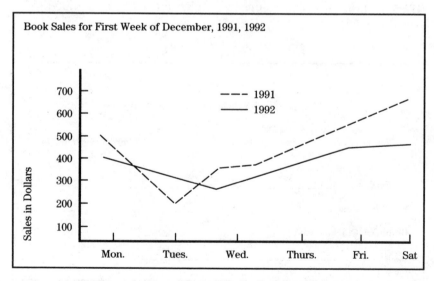

The bar chart is used to compare elements at a fixed point in time: for example, the comparative profits made by each department in a company. The bars can be horizontal or vertical, depending on the range of data. Bars can also be segmented to show different parts of the whole. As with a line chart, the scale for a bar chart should allow the data to spread out over the available space, not cram everything into one corner. In addition, make sure that the space between the bars differs from their width—it should be either greater or smaller. That way the bars will be easier to distinguish at a glance.

Bar Chart (vertical)

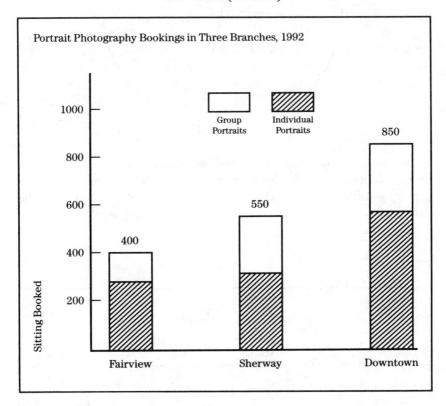

The pie chart is used to emphasize proportions—to draw attention to the relative size of the parts that make up a whole. For example, it can provide a quick visual comparison of individual department sales as a proportion of total sales. Visual separation by colour or shading can emphasize any particular piece of the pie.

Pie Chart
Appliance Profits, 1991

A matrix is another way of helping the reader to make comparisons, and is particularly useful for presenting an array of qualitative rather than quantitative information. A matrix can be used to highlight the different features of various alternatives, enabling the reader to make a choice.

Matrix

	Accommodation	Meals	Transportation	Extras	Cost
	10-Day Vacation Packages to London				
Plan 1 –	Double (shared) with bath	——	8-day pass. London Transport	Bus tour to Oxford	$1050 each
Plan 2 –	Double (shared)	Breakfast	——	——	$800 each
Plan 3 –	Single with bath	Breakfast	——	Tickets to 3 plays	$1000 each

Two dangers in illustrations

- Computer graphics programs make it possible to produce all kinds of fancy diagrams and enhancements of basic charts. They can add visual impact and even drama to your written material. But they do make it tempting to add so much detail that you obscure the basic data. Be sure that the designs you are creating are not too elaborate for your purpose. Visuals are meant not to dazzle but to make it easier for the reader to understand.
- Any illustration, whether done by hand or by computer, can distort information. For instance, the slope of a graph line can be made to look steep or shallow, even with the same data; trend lines can begin at a time that omits unfavourable periods. Although line and bar charts are the most susceptible to distortion, the shapes and proportions of other diagrams can also give a false picture. Be careful to present as accurate a picture as possible, so that your illustrations add to the credibility of your words.

7

Writing examinations

Most students feel nervous before tests and exams. It's not surprising. Writing an essay exam—even the open-book or take-home kind—imposes special pressures because both the time and the questions are restricted: you can't write and rewrite the way you can in a regular essay, and you must often write on topics you would otherwise choose to avoid. And although on the surface objective tests may look easier, because you don't have to compose the answers, they force you to be more decisive about your answers than essay exams do. You know that to do your best you need to feel calm—but how? These general guidelines will help you approach any test or exam with confidence. For special advice on open-book and take-home exams, see pp. 68-9; for objective tests, see p. 69.

Preparing for the exam

Review regularly
A weekly review of lecture notes and texts will help you not only to remember important material but to relate new information to old. If you don't review regularly, at the end of the year you'll be faced with relearning rather than remembering.

Set memory triggers
As you review, condense and focus the material by writing down in the margin key words or phrases that will trigger off a whole set of details in your mind. The trigger might be a concept word that names or points to an important theory or definition, or a quantitative phrase such as "three causes of the decline of manufacturing" or "five reasons for inflation."

Sometimes you can create an acronym or a nonsense sentence that will trigger an otherwise hard-to-remember set of facts—something like the acronym HOMES (Huron, Ontario, Michigan, Erie, Superior) for the Great Lakes. Since the difficulty of memorizing increases with the number of individual items you are trying to remember, any method that will reduce that number will increase your effectiveness.

Ask questions: try the three-C approach

Think of questions that will get to the heart of the material and cause you to examine the relations between various subjects or issues; then figure out how you would answer them. The three-C approach discussed on p. 8 may be a help. For example, reviewing the *components* of the subject could mean focusing on the main parts of an issue or on the definitions of major terms or theories. When reviewing *change* in the subject, you might ask yourself what elements caused it, directly or indirectly. To review *context* you might consider how certain aspects of the subject — issues, theories, actions, results — compare with others on the course. Essentially, what the three-C approach does is force you to look at the material from various perspectives.

Old examinations are useful both for seeing the type of question you might be asked and for checking on the thoroughness of your preparation. If old exams aren't available, you might get together with friends who are taking the same course and ask each other questions. Just remember that the most useful review questions are not the ones that require you to recall facts, but those that force you to analyse, integrate, or evaluate information.

Allow extra time

Give yourself lots of time to get to the exam. Nothing is more nerve-wracking than to think that you're going to be late. If you have to travel, don't forget that traffic can jam, and so can alarm clocks. Remember Murphy's Law: "Whatever can go wrong will." Anticipate any unusual difficulties and allow yourself a good margin.

Writing an essay exam

Read the exam

An exam is not a hundred-metre dash; instead of starting to write immediately, take time at the beginning to read through each question and create a plan of action. A few minutes spent on thinking and organizing will bring better results than the same time spent on writing a few more lines.

Allot your time

Reread the instructions carefully to find out how many questions you must answer and to see if you have any choice. Subtract five minutes or so for the initial planning, then divide the time you have left by the number of questions you have to answer. If possible, allow for a little extra time at the end to reread and edit your work. If the instructions on the exam indicate that not all questions are of equal value, apportion your time accordingly.

Choose your questions

Decide on the questions that you will do and the order in which you will do them. Your answers don't have to be in the same order as the questions. If you think you have lots of time, it's a good idea to place your best answer first, your worst answer in the middle, and your second best answer at the end, so that you leave the reader on a high note. If you think you will be rushed, though, it's wiser to work from best to worst. That way you will be sure to get all the marks you can on your good answers, and you won't have to cut a good answer short at the end.

Keep calm

If your first reaction on reading the exam is "I can't do any of it!" force yourself to keep calm; take ten slow, deep breaths as a deliberate relaxation exercise. Decide which is the question that you can answer best. Even if the exam seems disastrous at first, you can probably find one question that looks manageable: that's the one to begin with. It will get you rolling and increase your confidence. By the time you have finished, you are likely to find that your mind has worked through to the answer for another question.

Read each question carefully

As you turn to each question, read it again carefully and underline all the key words. The wording will probably suggest the number of parts your answer should have; be sure you don't overlook anything (a common mistake when people are nervous). Since the verb used in the question is usually a guide for the approach to take in your answer, it's especially important that you interpret the following terms correctly:

- *explain*: show the how's or why's;
- *compare*: give both similarities and differences—even if the question doesn't say *compare and contrast*;

- *outline*: state simply, without much development of each point (unless specifically asked);
- *discuss*: develop your points in an orderly way, taking into account contrary evidence or ideas.

Make notes
Before you even begin to organize your answer, jot down key ideas and information related to the topic on rough paper or the unlined pages of your answer book. These notes will save you the worry of forgetting something by the time you begin writing. Next, arrange those parts you want to use into a brief plan.

Be direct
Get to the points quickly and illustrate them frequently. In an exam, as opposed to an essay, it's best to use a direct approach. Don't worry about composing a graceful introduction: simply state the main points that you are going to discuss, then get on with developing them. Remember that your paper will likely be one of many read and marked by someone who has to work quickly—the clearer your answers are, the better they will be received.

For each main point give the kind of specific details that will prove you really know the material. General statements will show you are able to assimilate information, but they need examples to back them up.

Write legibly
Writing that's hard to read produces a cranky reader. When the marker has to struggle to decipher your ideas, you may get poorer results than you deserve. If for some special reason (such as a physical handicap) your writing is hard to read, see if you can make special arrangements to use a typewriter. If your writing is just plain bad, it's probably better to print.

Write on alternate lines
Writing on every other line will not only make your writing easier to read, but leave you space for changes and additions; you won't have to cover your paper with a lot of messy circles and arrows.

Keep to your time plan
Keep to your plan and don't skip any questions. Try to write something on each topic. Remember that it's easier to score half marks for a question you don't know much about than it is to score full marks for

one you could write pages on. If you find yourself running out of time on an answer and still haven't finished, summarize the remaining points and go on to the next question. Leave a large space between questions so that you can go back and add more if you have time. If you write a new ending, remember to cross out the old one—neatly.

Reread your answers

No matter how tired or fed up you are, reread your answers at the end, if there's time. Check especially for clarity of expression; try to get rid of confusing sentences and increase the logical connections between your ideas. Revisions that make answers easier to read are always worth the effort.

Writing an open-book exam

If you think that permission to take your books into the exam room is an "Open Sesame" to success, be forewarned. You could fall into the trap of relying too heavily on them; you may spend so much time riffling through pages and looking things up that you won't have time to write good answers. The result may be worse than if you had been allowed no books at all.

If you want to do well, use your books only to check information and look up specific, hard-to-remember details for a topic you already know a good deal about. For instance, if your subject is history you can look up exact dates or quotations; for economics you can look up statistics; for an exam in social theory you can check some classical references and find the authors' exact definitions of key concepts—if you know where to find them quickly. In other words, use the books to make sure your answers are precise and well illustrated. Never use them to replace studying and careful exam preparation.

Writing a take-home exam

The benefit of a take-home exam is that you have time to plan your answers and to consult your texts or other sources. The catch is that the time is usually less than it would be for an ordinary essay. Don't work yourself into a frenzy trying to respond with a polished research essay for each question; rather, use the extra time to create a well-written exam answer. Keep in mind that you were given this assignment to test your overall command of the course: your reader is likely to be less concerned with your specialized research than with evidence that you have understood and assimilated the material.

The guidelines for a take-home exam are therefore similar to those for a regular exam; the only difference is that you don't need to keep such a close eye on the clock:

1. Keep your introduction short and get to the point quickly.

2. Have a straightforward and obvious organizational pattern so that the reader can easily see your main ideas.

3. Use frequent concrete examples to back up your points.

4. Where possible, show the range of your knowledge of course material by referring to a number of different sources, rather than constantly using the same ones.

5. Try to show that you can analyse and evaluate material: that you can do more than simply repeat information.

Writing an objective test

Objective tests are common in the social sciences. Although sometimes the questions are the true-false kind, most often they are multiple-choice. The main difficulty with these tests is that their questions are designed to confuse the student who is not certain of the correct answers. If you are one of those people who are forever second-guessing themselves, or who readily see two sides to every question, you may find objective tests particularly hard at first. Fortunately, practice almost always improves performance.

Preparation for objective tests is the same as for other kinds. Here, though, it's especially important to pay attention to definitions and unexpected or confusing pieces of information, because they can so readily be adapted to make objective-test questions. Although there is no sure recipe for doing well on an objective test — other than knowing the course material completely and confidently — these suggestions may help you to do better:

Find out the marking system
If marks are based solely on the number of right answers, you should pick an answer for every question even if you aren't sure it's the right one. For a true-false question you have a 50-per-cent chance that it will be; and even for a multiple-choice question with four possible answers, you would on average get 25 per cent right if you picked the answers blindfolded.

On the other hand, if there is a penalty for wrong answers—if marks are deducted for errors—you should guess only when you are fairly sure you are right, or when you are able to rule out most of the possibilities. Don't make wild guesses.

Do the easy questions first

Go through the test at least twice. On the first round, don't waste time on troublesome questions. Since the questions are usually of equal value, it's best to get all the marks you can on the ones you find easy. You can tackle the more difficult questions on the next round. This approach has two advantages:

1. You won't be forced, because you have run out of time, to leave out any questions that you could easily have answered correctly.

2. When you come back to a difficult question on the second round, you may find that in the meantime you have figured out the answer.

Make your guesses educated ones

If you have decided to guess, at least increase your chances of getting the answers right. Forget about intuition, hunches, and lucky numbers. More important, forget about so-called patterns of correct answers—the idea that if there have been two "A" answers in a row, the next one can't possibly be "A," or that if there hasn't been a "true" for a while, "true" must be a good guess. Unfortunately, many test-setters either don't worry about patterns at all, or else deliberately elude pattern-hunters by giving the right answer the same letter or number several times in a row.

Remember that constructing good objective tests is a special skill that not all instructors have mastered. Often the questions they pose, though sound enough as questions, do not produce enough realistic alternatives for answers. In such cases the test-setter may resort to some less-realistic options, and if you keep your eyes open you can spot them. James F. Shepherd[1] has suggested a number of tips that will increase your chances of making the right guess:

- Start by weeding out all the answers you know are wrong, rather than looking for the right one.
- Avoid any terms you don't recognize. Some students are taken in by anything that looks like sophisticated terminology and may assume that such answers must be correct. They are usually wrong: the unfamiliar term may well be a red herring, especially if it is close in sound to the correct one.

- Avoid extremes. Most often the right answer lies in between. For example, suppose that the options are the numbers 800,000; 350,000; 275,000; and 15: the highest and lowest numbers are likely to be wrong.
- Avoid absolutes, especially on questions dealing with people. Few aspects of human life are as certain as is implied by such words as *everyone*, *all*, or *no one*; *always*, *invariably*, or *never*. Statements containing these words are usually false.
- Avoid jokes or humorous statements.
- Avoid demeaning or insulting statements. Like jokes, these are usually inserted simply to provide a full complement of options.
- Choose the best available answer, even if it is not indisputably true.
- Choose the long answer over the short (it's more likely to contain the detail needed to make it correct) and the particular statement over the general (generalizations are usually too sweeping to be true).
- Choose "all of the above" over individual answers. Test-setters know that students with a patchy knowledge of the course material will often fasten on the one fact they know. Only those with a thorough knowledge will recognize that all the answers listed are correct.

Two final tips

If you have time at the end of the exam, go back and reread the questions. One or two wrong answers caused by misreading can make a significant difference to your score. On the other hand, don't start second-guessing yourself and changing a lot of answers at the last minute. Studies have shown that when students make changes they are often wrong. Stick to your decisions unless you know for certain that you have made a mistake.

Notes

[1] James F. Shepherd, *College Study Skills* (Boston: Houghton Mifflin, 1979) and *RSVP: The Houghton Mifflin Reading, Study, and Vocabulary Program* (Boston: Houghton Mifflin, 1981).

8

Writing a résumé and letter

of application

Whether you are looking for a summer job, applying to graduate school, or seeking permanent employment, eventually you will have to write a résumé and letter of application. They may also be needed for some courses, including those with work-study options. The person who reads your application will not have time to read reams of material, so you will need to be brief yet precise.

Preparing a standard résumé

Think of a résumé not just as a summary of facts but as a selling tool, designed to fit an organization's needs. You will need to supply some basic information, but how you organize and emphasize it is up to you. One good organizing principle is to put your most important qualifications first, so that they are noticed at first glance. For most students this means leading with educational qualifications, but for others it may mean starting with work experience. Within each section, use reverse chronological order, so that the most recent item is at the beginning.

Whatever arrangement you choose, your goal is to keep the résumé as concise as possible while including all the specific information that will help to "sell" you. A reader will lose interest in a résumé that goes on and on, mixing the significant with the trivial. On the other hand, what may seem to a student to be irrelevant can in fact demonstrate a sense of responsibility or willingness to work hard. For example, working as a part-time short-order cook may be significant if you state that that was how you paid your way through university.

Here is a list of common résumé information, with some suggestions on how to present it:

Name. Usually in capital letters and centred at the top of the page.

Address and telephone number. These can come at the top or bottom of the page. If you have a temporary student address, remember to state where you can be reached at other times.

Objective (optional). It's often helpful to let the employer know your career goal, or at least your current aim for employment. (Example: a junior planning position with opportunity for advancement.)

Education. Include any degrees and related diplomas or certifications, along with the institution that granted them and the date. If it will help your case, and you are short of other qualifications, you may also list courses you have taken that are relevant to the job.

Awards or honours. These may be in a separate section or included with Education.

Work experience. Give the name and location of the employer, along with your job title and the dates of employment. Instead of outlining your duties (which an employee may or may not carry out well), list your accomplishments on the job, using point form and action verbs. For example:

• designed and administered a public awareness survey;
• supervised a three-member field crew.

Research experience or special skills. This is a chance to list information that may give you an advantage in a competitive market, such as experience with computers, or knowledge of a second language. If you have worked as a research assistant, be sure to state the type of work you did and whom you worked for. (Example: Assisted Professor Julian Somers in a laboratory research project on "The Liquid Limit of Leda Clay," Carleton University, summer 1991.)

Other interests (optional). Depending on the amount of information you already need to include, and on the type of employer, you may choose to omit this section. Sometimes, however, including a few achievements or interests, such as athletic or musical accomplishment, will show that you are well-rounded or specially disciplined. In any case, avoid a long list of items that merely show passive or minimal involvement.

References (optional). If asked to supply the names of people who can give references, be sure to give the complete title, address, and phone number of each one. If you are not asked for references, you don't need to supply names. Increasingly, employers are waiting until they are serious about hiring an individual before they consider references. If you do supply names, check beforehand with those named, as a courtesy.

Standard Résumé

MARTIN SOMERS

until April 1992:	home address:
123 College Rd.	45 Main St.
Toronto, Ontario M2M 2M2	Ottawa, Ontario K1K 1K1
tel: (416) 123-4567	tel: (613) 456-0000

Employment Goal: an entry position in the pulp and paper industry, in field research or administration, where my background in environmental studies and geography would be useful.

Education
• MSc in Environmental Studies, York University, expected in May 1992
  (Thesis: "The Links Between Government Policy and Forest Clearance in British Columbia")
• BA (Honours Geography) Carleton University, 1990

Honours and Awards
• Dean's List, 1988-89, 1989-90, Carleton University
• Cailey Award as top student in Geography, 1989

Work Experience
Summer 1991 Research Assistant for Professor Gary Smithers in field study of "Perceptions of Place in a Rural-Urban Fringe Environment", in Mexico.
— helped develop questionnaire and conduct interviews;
— prepared statistical analysis of findings.
Summer 1990 Head of tree-planting crew for Planters Inc. in Northern Ontario
— hired, trained and supervised crew of eight planters;
— organized delivery of equipment and food supplies;
— managed budget and kept accounts.
Summers, Member of tree-planting crew for Planters Inc.
1987-90 Earned enough to pay my way through university.

Other Skills, Interests and Achievements
• skilled in air photo interpretation and computer-assisted cartography
• Captain of Carleton University hockey team, 1989-90
• served as Big Brother in Toronto since August, 1990

A résumé with these traditional categories is not the only kind that works, however. Even if your experience is not directly related to the position you want, you can still write an effective functional résumé. Most functional résumés have categories for experience in different functions (for example: Research, Administration, Sales). Others may focus on personal attributes such as initiative, teamwork, analytic ability, or communication skills. If you chose to write a functional résumé, it's a good idea to include at the bottom a brief record of employment with dates, so that the reader has a firm grasp of when you did what.

Functional résumé

REBECCA McLEAN

16 Harbour St.
Halifax, Nova Scotia B3H 2L4
tel: (902) 491-3020

Job Objective: Work in promotions or fundraising area in a public-sector organization.

Profile: An energetic, bilingual communicator, with a record of initiative.

Communication Skills:
- B.A., Honours, in English, Dalhousie University, June, 1992; B + average.
- Sport & Entertainment editor for Dalhousie student newspaper, 1991-92. Reporter, 1990-91.
- debated regularly as a member of Dalhousie's Debating Society.
- volunteer tour guide for university, summer, 1990-91.
- fluent in French, both written and spoken.

Initiative:
- founded my own dried flower business, Flower Fancies, when still in school (1986-88). Designed and sold arrangements, and kept accounts, earning enough to pay for my first year at Dalhousie.
- organized with two other students an environmental awareness week at university (1991). Responsible for enlisting and managing 20 volunteers.

Other Achievements & Activities:
- member of Dalhousie tennis team (1989-91)
- play the guitar and enjoy singing

References
1. Professor James Stark, Dalhousie University, Department of English, Halifax, N.S. B3H 3J5
2. Mrs. Mabel Williams, Student Affairs Director, Dalhousie University.

The tone of a résumé should be up-beat, so don't draw attention to any potential weaknesses you may have, such as a lack of experience in a particular area. Never list a category and then write "None" — you don't want to suggest that you lack something! Remember to re-order your list of special skills to suggest a fit with each particular job you apply for, so that the reader will see at a glance that you have the needed skills. Finally, never claim more for yourself than is true; putting a falsehood into a résumé can be grounds for firing if it is discovered later.

You are not required to state anything about age, place of birth, race, religion, or gender. (Use of initials, rather than your given name, may hide the latter.) Of course, if you feel it would be to your advantage to include any or all of these items, do so. And keep in mind that if you are completing an application form with set questions, it is a good idea to provide all the information requested (especially about age and gender); if you don't, your application may be ignored.

Letter of application for a job

Do *not* use the same letter for all applications: craft each one to focus directly on the particular job and company in question and catch the attention of each particular reader. In a sense, both the résumé and the letter of application are intended to open the door to the next stage in job-seeking: the interview. The key is to link your skills to the position, not just to state information. What matters is not what *you want* but what the *employer needs*.

One challenge in writing a latter of application is to tell about yourself and your qualifications without seeming egotistical. Two tips can help:

1. Limit sentences beginning with "I." Instead, try burying some I's in the middle of a sentence, where they will be less noticeable. (Example: For two months last summer, I worked as . . .)

2. Avoid, as much as possible, making unsupported, subjective claims. Instead of saying "I am a highly skilled manager", say something like "Last summer I managed a $50,000 field study with a crew of seven assistants." Rather than claim "I have excellent research skills," you might say, "Based on my previous work, Professor Sam Jonas selected me from ten applicants to help in his summer research work."

Here is an example (not to be copied rigidly) of an application letter that tries to connect the applicant's background with the needs of the company:

> Your advertisement in the Ottawa Journal for a Junior Environmental
> Officer caught my attention, since my qualifications match those you

are seeking. As a graduating student in Environmental Studies at Carleton University, I would like to apply for the position and have enclosed a résumé.

Beyond my specialist academic program, I have had relevant environmental field experience. For two summers, I worked with Professor Susan LeClerc in her studies of wetland pollution south of Georgian Bay, helping both in the laboratory and in the wetlands south of James Bay. I also enjoy and am used to the kind of outdoor work you require. In my first summer as a university student, I worked as a tree-planter in harsh conditions in northern British Columbia. In addition, I am able to speak French well enough to converse with your French-speaking clients in Ontario and Quebec.

I would appreciate the chance to discuss with you further how I could contribute to Outland Developments, and will call you next week to see if it is convenient to arrange an interview.

Of course, your application package will be judged not just by what you say but also by how you say it. Take the time to double-check for grammar and spelling errors, and make sure that the layout is clear and looks professional. With applications, as with job interviews, first impressions count.

9

Writing with style

Writing with style does not mean stuffing your prose with fancy words and extravagant images. Any style, from the simplest to the most elaborate, can be effective depending on the occasion and intent. Writers known for their style are those who have projected something of their own personality into their writing; we can hear a distinctive voice in what they say. Obviously it takes time to develop a unique style. To begin, you have to decide what general effect you want to create.

Taste in style reflects the times. In earlier centuries, when few people outside the leisure class ever had a chance to read, many respected writers wrote in an elaborate style that we would think much too wordy. Now almost all of us read, but newspapers, television, and radio compete with books for our attention, and as a result we tend to favour a simpler kind of writing. Journalists have led the trend towards short, easy-to-grasp sentences and paragraphs. Writing in an academic context, you may expect your audience to be more reflective than the average newspaper reader, but the most effective style is still one that is clear, concise, and forceful.

Be clear

Since sentence structure is dealt with in Chapter 10, this section will focus on clear wording and paragraphing.

Choose clear words

A good dictionary is a wise investment; get into the habit of using one. It will give you not only common meanings, but less familiar applications, archaic uses, and derivations, as well as proper spelling. Canadian usage and spelling may follow either British or American practices, but usually combine aspects of both; you should check before you buy a dictionary to ensure that it gives the variants.

A thesaurus lists words that are closely related in meaning. It can help when you want to avoid repeating yourself, or when you are fumbling for a word that's on the tip of your tongue. But be careful: make sure you remember the difference between denotative and connotative meanings. A word's denotation is its primary or "dictionary" meaning. Its connotations are any associations that it may suggest; they may not be as exact as the denotations, but they are part of the impression the word conveys. If you examine a list of "synonyms" in a thesaurus, you will see that even words with similar meanings can have dramatically different connotations. For example, alongside the word *indifferent* your thesaurus may give the following: *neutral*, *unconcerned*, *careless*, *easy-going*, *unambitious*, and *half-hearted*. Imagine the different impressions you would create if you chose one or the other of those words to complete this sentence: "Questioned about the experiment's chance of success, he was _____ in his response." In order to write clearly, you must remember that a reader may react to the suggestive meaning of a word as much as to its "dictionary" meaning.

Use plain English

Plain words are almost always more forceful than fancy ones. If you aren't sure what plain English is, think of everyday speech: how do you talk to your friends? Many of our most common words — the ones that sound most natural and direct — are short. A good number of them are also among the oldest words in the English language. By contrast, most of the words that English has derived from other languages are longer and more complicated; even after they've been used for centuries, they can still sound artificial. For this reason you should beware of words loaded with prefixes (*pre-*, *post-*, *anti-*, *pro-*, *sub-*, *maxi-*, etc.) and suffixes (*-ate*, *-ize*, *-tion*, etc.). These Latinate attachments can make individual words more precise and efficient, but putting a lot of them together will make your writing seem dense and hard to understand. In many cases you can substitute a plain word for a fancy one:

Fancy	*Plain*
determinant	cause
utilization	use
cognizant	aware

obviate	prevent
terminate	end
infuriate	anger
oration	speech
conclusion	end
requisite	needed
numerous	many
finalize	finish, complete
systematize	order
sanitize	clean
remuneration	pay
maximization	increase

Suggesting that you write in plain English does not mean that you should never pick an unfamiliar, long, or foreign word: sometimes those words are the only ones that will convey precisely what you mean. Inserting an unusual expression into a passage of plain writing can also be an effective means of catching the reader's attention — as long as you don't do it too often.

Be precise

Always be as precise or exact as you can. Avoid all-purpose adjectives like *major*, *significant*, and *important*, and vague verbs such as *involve*, *entail*, and *exist*, when you can be more specific:

orig . Donald Smith was involved in the construction of the CPR.

rev. Donald Smith helped finance the construction of the CPR.

Here's another example:

orig . Granting public-service employees the right to strike was a significant legacy of Lester Pearson's years as Prime Minister.

rev. Granting public-service employees the right to strike was a costly legacy of Lester Pearson's years as Prime Minister.

(or)

rev. Granting public-service employees the right to strike was a beneficial legacy of Lester Pearson's years as Prime Minister.

Avoid unnecessary qualifiers

Qualifiers such as *very*, *rather*, and *extremely* are over-used. Experienced writers know that saying something is *very beautiful* may have less impact than saying simply that it is *beautiful*. For example, compare these sentences:

> That is a beautiful garden.
> That is a very beautiful garden.

Which has more punch?

When you think that an adjective needs qualifying—and sometimes it will—first see if it's possible to change either the adjective or the phrasing. Instead of writing

> Imperial Castings made a very big profit last year

write

> Imperial Castings made an unprecedented profit last year

or (if you aren't sure whether or not the profit actually set a record):

> Imperial Castings' profit rose forty per cent last year.

In some cases qualifiers not only weaken your writing but are redundant, since the adjectives themselves are absolutes. To say that something is *very unique* makes as much—or as little—sense as to say that someone is *rather pregnant* or *very dead*.

Avoid fancy jargon

All academic subjects have their own terminology; it may be unfamiliar to outsiders, but it helps specialists to explain things to each other. The trouble is that people sometimes use jargon—special, technical language—unnecessarily, thinking it will make them seem more knowledgeable. Too often the result is not clarity, but complication. The guideline is easy: use specialized terminology only when it's a kind of shorthand that will help you explain something more precisely and efficiently. If plain prose will do just as well, stick to it.

Creating clear paragraphs

Paragraphs come in so many sizes and patterns that no single formula could possibly cover them all. The two basic principles to remember are these: (1) a paragraph is a means of developing and framing an idea or impression, and (2) the divisions between paragraphs aren't random, but indicate a shift in focus.

Develop your ideas

You are not likely to sit down and consciously ask yourself "What pattern shall I use to develop this paragraph?" What comes first is the idea you intend to develop: the pattern the paragraph takes should flow from the idea itself and the way you want to discuss or expand it. (The most common ways of developing an idea are outlined on pp. 19-22.)

You may take one or several paragraphs to develop an idea fully. For a definition alone you could write one paragraph or ten, depending on the complexity of the subject and the nature of the assignment. Just remember that ideas need development, and that each new paragraph signals a change in idea.

Consider the topic sentence

Skilled skim-readers know that they can get the general drift of a book simply by reading the first sentence of each paragraph. The reason is that most paragraphs begin by stating the central idea to be developed. If you are writing your essay from a formal plan, you will probably find that each section and subsection will generate the topic sentence for a new paragraph.

Like the thesis statement for the essay as a whole, the topic sentence is not obligatory: in some paragraphs the controlling idea is not stated until the middle or even the end, and in others it is not stated at all but merely implied. Nevertheless, it's a good idea to think out a topic sentence for every paragraph. That way you'll be sure that each one has a readily graspable point and is clearly connected to what comes before and after. When revising your initial draft, check to see that each paragraph is held together by a topic sentence, either stated or implied. If you find that you can't formulate one, you should probably rework the whole paragraph.

Maintain focus

To be clear, a paragraph should contain only those details that are in some way related to the central idea. It must also be structured so that the details are easily *seen* to be related. One way of showing these relations is to keep the same grammatical subject in most of the sentences that make up the paragraph. When the grammatical subject keeps shifting, a paragraph loses focus, as in the following example:[1]

> Students in high school play a variety of sports these days. In the fall, football still attracts many, although an increasing number now play soccer. For some basketball is the favourite when the fall season is over, but you will find that swimming, volleyball and gymnastics are also popular. Cold winter temperatures may allow the school to have an outdoor rink, and then hockey and skating become a source of enjoyment for many. In spring, though, the rinks begin melting, and so

> there is less opportunity to play. Then some students take up soccer
> again, while track and field, baseball or tennis also attract many
> participants.

Here the grammatical subject (underlined) is constantly jumping from
one thing to another. Notice how much stronger the focus becomes
when all the sentences have the same grammatical subject — either
the same noun, a synonym, or a related pronoun:

> Students in high school play a variety of sports these days. In the fall,
> many still choose football, although an increasing number now play
> soccer. When the fall season is over, some turn to basketball; others
> prefer swimming, volleyball or gymnastics. If cold winter temperatures
> permit an outdoor rink, many students enjoy hockey or skating. Once
> the ice begins to melt in spring, though, they can play less often. Then
> some take up soccer again, while others choose track and field,
> baseball or tennis.

Naturally it's not always possible to retain the same grammatical
subject throughout a paragraph. If you were comparing the athletic
pursuits of boys and girls, for example, you would have to switch back
and forth between boys and girls as your grammatical subject. In the
same way, you will have to shift when you are discussing examples of
an idea or exceptions to it.

Avoid monotony

If most or all of the sentences in your paragraph have the same grammatical subject, how do you avoid boring your reader? There are two
easy ways:

Use stand-in words.   Pronouns, either personal (*I, we, you, he,
she, it, they*) or demonstrative (*this, that, those*), can stand in for the
subject, as can synonyms (words or phrases that mean the same thing).
The revised paragraph on students' sports, for example, uses the pronouns *some, most,* and *they* as substitutes for *students.* Most well-
written paragraphs have a liberal sprinkling of these stand-in words.

"Bury" the subject by putting something in front of it.
When the subject is placed in the middle of the sentence rather than at
the beginning, it's less obvious to the reader. If you take another look
at the revised paragraph, you'll see that in several sentences there is a
word or phrase in front of the subject, giving the paragraph a feeling of
variety. Even a single word, such as *first, then, lately,* or *moreover,*
will do the trick.

Link your ideas

To create coherent paragraphs, you need to link your ideas clearly. Linking words are those connectors—conjunctions and conjunctive adverbs—that show the *relations* between one sentence, or part of a sentence, and another; they're also known as transition words, because they bridge the transition from one thought to another. Make a habit of using linking words when you shift from one grammatical subject or idea to another, whether the shift occurs within a single paragraph or as you move from one paragraph to the next. Here are some of the most common connectors and the logical relations they indicate:

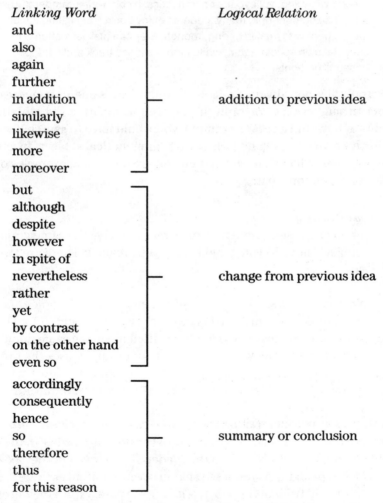

Linking Word	*Logical Relation*
and	
also	
again	
further	
in addition	addition to previous idea
similarly	
likewise	
more	
moreover	
but	
although	
despite	
however	
in spite of	
nevertheless	change from previous idea
rather	
yet	
by contrast	
on the other hand	
even so	
accordingly	
consequently	
hence	
so	summary or conclusion
therefore	
thus	
for this reason	

Numerical terms such as *first*, *second*, and *third* also work well as links.

Vary the length, but avoid extremes

Ideally, academic writing will have a comfortable balance of long and short paragraphs. Avoid the extremes, especially the one-sentence paragraph, which can only state an idea, without explaining or developing it. A series of very short paragraphs is usually a sign that you have not developed your ideas in enough detail, or that you have started new paragraphs unnecessarily. On the other hand, a succession of long paragraphs can be tiring and difficult to read. In deciding when to start a new paragraph, remember always to consider what is clearest and most helpful for the reader.

Be concise

At one time or another, you will probably be tempted to pad your writing. Whatever the reason—because you need to write two or three thousand words and have only enough to say for one thousand, or just because you think length is strength and hope to get a better mark for the extra—padding is a mistake.

Strong writing is always concise. It leaves out anything that does not serve some communicative or stylistic purpose, in order to say as much as possible in as few words as possible. Concise writing will help you do better on both your essays and your exams.

Guidelines for concise writing

1. Use adverbs and adjectives sparingly

Avoid the shot-gun approach to adverbs and adjectives; don't just spray your work with modifiers in the hope that one will hit. One well-chosen word is always better than a series of synonyms:

orig. As well as being costly and financially extravagant, the venture is reckless and foolhardy.

rev. The venture is foolhardy as well as costly.

2. Avoid noun clusters

A recent trend in some writing is to use nouns as adjectives, as in the phrase *noun clusters*. This device can be effective occasionally, but frequent use can produce a monstrous pile-up of words. Breaking up noun clusters may not always produce fewer words, but it will make your writing easier to read:

orig. word-processor utilization manual

rev. manual for using word-processors

orig. pollution investigation committee
rev. committee to investigate pollution

3. Avoid chains of relative clauses

Sentences full of clauses beginning with *which, that,* or *who* are usually more wordy than necessary. Try reducing some of those clauses to phrases or single words:

orig. The solutions which were discussed last night have a practical benefit which is easily grasped by people who have no technical training.

rev. The solutions discussed last night have a practical benefit, easily grasped by non-technical people.

4. Try reducing clauses to phrases or words

Independent clauses can often be reduced by subordination. Here are a few examples:

orig. The report was written in a clear and concise manner and it was widely read.

better Written in a clear and concise manner, the report was widely read.

best Clear and concise, the report was widely read.

orig. His plan was of a radical nature and was a source of embarrassment to his employer.

rev. His radical plan embarrassed his employer.

For more detail on subordination and reduction, see p. 89.

5. Strike out hackneyed expressions and circumlocutions

Trite or roundabout phrases may flow from your pen without a thought, but they make for stale prose. Unnecessary words are deadwood; be prepared to hunt and chop ruthlessly to keep your writing vital:

Wordy	Revised
due to the fact that	because
at this point in time	now
consensus of opinion	consensus
in the near future	soon
when all is said and done	(omit)
in the eventuality that	if
in all likelihood	likely
it could be said that	possibly, maybe
in all probability	probably

6. Avoid "it is" and "there is" beginnings

When possible, try to avoid *it is* or *there is* (*are*) beginnings. Your sentences will be crisper and more concise:

orig. There is little time remaining for the sales manager to reverse the financial trend.

rev. Little time remains for the sales manager to reverse the financial trend.

orig. It is certain that pollution will increase.

rev. Pollution will certainly increase.

Be forceful

Developing a forceful, vigorous style simply means learning some common tricks of the trade and practising them until they become habit.

Choose active over passive verbs

An active verb creates more energy than a passive one does:

Active: She threw the ball.

Passive: The ball was thrown by her.

Moreover, passive constructions tend to produce awkward, convoluted phrasing. Writers of bureaucratic documents are among the worst offenders:

> It has been decided that the utilization of small rivers in the province for purposes of generating hydro-electric power should be studied by our department and that a report to the Deputy should be made by our Director as soon as possible.

The passive verbs in this mouthful make it hard to tell who is doing what.

Passive verbs are appropriate in four instances:

1. When the subject is the passive recipient of some action:

> The cabinet minister was heckled by the angry crowd.

2. When you want to emphasize the object rather than the person acting:

> The anti-pollution devices in all three plants will be improved.

3. When you want to avoid an awkward shift of subject in a sentence or paragraph. Using the passive will sometimes help you maintain focus:

> The Jesuits began to convert the Hurons but <u>were attacked</u> by the Iroquois band before they had completed the mission.

4. When you want to avoid placing responsibility or blame:

> Several errors <u>were made</u> in the calculations.

When these exceptions don't apply, make an effort to use active verbs for a livelier style.

Use personal subjects

Most of us find it more interesting to learn about people than about things—hence the enduring appeal of the gossip columns. Wherever possible, therefore, make the subjects of your sentences personal. This trick goes hand-in-hand with use of active verbs. Almost any sentence becomes more lively with active verbs and a personal subject:

> *orig.* The <u>outcome</u> of the union members' vote <u>was</u> the <u>decision</u> to resume work on Monday.

> *rev.* The union <u>members voted</u> to return to work on Monday.

Here's another example:

> *orig.* It can be <u>assumed</u> that an <u>agreement was reached</u>, since <u>there were</u> smiles on both management and union sides when the <u>meeting was finished</u>.

> *rev.* <u>We can assume</u> that <u>management and the union reached</u> an agreement, since both <u>bargainers were smiling</u> when <u>they finished</u> the meeting.

(or)

> *rev.* Apparently <u>management and union reached</u> an agreement since, when <u>they finished</u> the meeting, both <u>bargainers were smiling</u>.

Use concrete details

Concrete details are easier to understand—and to remember—than abstract theories. Whenever you are discussing abstract concepts, therefore, always provide specific examples and illustrations; if you have a choice between a concrete word and an abstract one, choose the concrete. Consider this sentence:

> The French explored the northern territory and traded with the native people.

Now see how a few specific details can bring the facts to life:

> The French voyageurs paddled their way along the river systems of the
> north, trading their blankets and copper kettles for the Indians' furs.

Suggesting that you add concreteness doesn't mean getting rid of all abstractions. It's simply a plea to balance them with accurate details. Here is one instance in which added wording, if it is concrete and correct, can improve your writing.

Make important ideas stand out

Experienced writers know how to manipulate sentences in order to emphasize certain points. Here are some of their techniques:

Place key words in strategic positions

The positions of emphasis in a sentence are the beginning and, above all, the end. If you want to bring your point home with force, don't put the key words in the middle of the sentence. Save them for the last:

orig. People are less afraid of losing wealth than of losing face in this image-conscious society.

rev. In this image-conscious society, people are less afraid of losing wealth than of losing face.

Subordinate minor ideas

Small children connect incidents with a string of *ands*, as if everything were of equal importance:

> We went to the zoo and we saw a lion and John spilled his drink.

As they grow up, however, they learn to subordinate: that is, to make one part of a sentence less important in order to emphasize another point:

> Because the bus was delayed, we missed our class.

Major ideas stand out more and connections become clearer when minor ideas are subordinated:

orig. Night came and the ship slipped away from her captors.

rev. When night came, the ship slipped away from her captors.

Make your most important idea the subject of the main clause, and try to put it at the end, where it will be most emphatic:

orig. I was relieved when I saw my marks.

rev. When I saw my marks, I was relieved.

Vary sentence structure

As with anything else, variety adds spice to writing. One way of adding variety, which will also make an important idea stand out, is to use a periodic rather than a simple sentence structure.

Most sentences follow the simple pattern of subject — verb — object (plus modifiers):

> The <u>dog</u> <u>bit</u> the <u>man</u>.
>   s   v   o

> The <u>startled</u> <u>dog</u> <u>bit</u> the <u>man</u> <u>on the ankle</u>.
>   m   s   v   o   m

A *simple sentence* such as this gives the main idea at the beginning and therefore creates little tension. A *periodic sentence*, on the other hand, does not give the main clause until the end, following one or more subordinate clauses:

> Since he had failed to keep his promises or to inspire the voters, in the next election <u>he</u> <u>was defeated</u>.
>   s   v

The longer the periodic sentence is, the greater the suspense and the more emphatic the final part. Since this high-tension structure is more difficult to read than the simple sentence, your readers would be exhausted if you used it too often. Save it for those times when you want to create a special effect or play on emotions.

Vary sentence length

A short sentence can add punch to an important point, especially when it comes as a surprise. This technique can be particularly useful for conclusions. Don't overdo it, though. A string of long sentences may be monotonous, but a string of short ones has a staccato effect that can make your writing sound like a child's reader: "This is my dog. See him run."

Still, academic papers usually have too many long sentences rather than too many short ones. Since short sentences are easier to read, try breaking up clusters of long ones. Check any sentence over 20 words or so to see if it will benefit from being split.

Use contrast

Just as a jeweller will highlight a diamond by displaying it against dark velvet, so you can highlight an idea by placing it against a contrasting background:

orig. Most employees in industry do not have indexed pensions.

rev. Unlike civil servants, most employees in industry do not have indexed pensions.

Using parallel phrasing will increase the effect of the contrast:

Although he often spoke to business groups, he seldom spoke in Parliament.

Use a well-placed adverb or correlative construction

Adding an adverb or two can sometimes help you to dramatize a concept:

orig. Although I dislike the proposal, I must accept it as the practical answer.

rev. Although emotionally I dislike the concept, intellectually I must accept it as the practical answer.

Correlatives such as *both . . . and* or *not only . . . but also* can be used to emphasize combinations as well:

orig. Smith was a good coach and a good friend.

rev. Smith was both a good coach and a good friend.
rev. Smith was not only a good coach but also a good friend.

Use repetition

Repetition is a highly effective emphatic device. It helps to stir the emotions:

He fought injustice and corruption. He fought complacent politicians and inept policies. He fought hard, but he always fought fairly.

Of course, you would only use such a dramatic technique on rare occasions.

Use your ears

Your ears are probably your best critics: make good use of them. Before producing a final copy of any piece of writing, read it out loud, in a clear voice. The difference between cumbersome and fluent passages will be unmistakable.

Some final advice: write before you revise

No one would expect you to sit down and put all this advice into practice as soon as you start to write. You would feel so constrained that it would be hard to get anything down on paper at all. You will be better off if you begin practising these techniques during the editing process, when you are looking critically at what you have already written. Some experienced writers can combine the creative and critical functions, but most of us find it easier to write a rough draft first, before starting the detailed task of revising.

Note
[1]Discussion of focus based on Robert Cluett and Lee Ahlborn, *Effective English Prose* (New York: L.W. Singer, 1965), 51.

10

Common errors in grammar

and usage

This chapter is not a comprehensive grammar lesson: it's simply a survey of those areas where students most often make mistakes. It will help you to keep a look-out for weaknesses as you are editing your work. Once you get into the habit of checking, it won't be long before you are correcting potential problems as you write.

The grammatical terms used here are the most simple and familiar ones; if you need to review some of them, see the glossary. For a thorough treatment of grammar or usage, consult a complete text such as A.J. Thompson and A.V. Martinet's *A Practical English Grammar*, 3rd ed. (Oxford: Oxford University Press, 1980).

Troubles with sentence unity

Sentence fragments
To be complete, a sentence must have both a subject and a verb in an independent clause; if it doesn't, it's a fragment. Occasionally a sentence fragment is acceptable, as in

   ✓ Will the government try to abolish the Senate? <u>Not likely.</u>

Here the sentence fragment *not likely* is clearly intended to be understood as a short form of *It is not likely that it will try*. Unintentional sentence fragments, on the other hand, usually seem incomplete rather than shortened:

   ✗ I enjoy living in Vancouver. <u>Being a skier who likes the sea.</u>

The last "sentence" is incomplete: where is the subject or verb? (Remember that a participle such as *being* is not a verb; "-ing" words by themselves are only verbals or part-verbs.) The fragment can be made into a complete sentence by adding a subject and a verb:

✓   I am a skier who likes the sea.

Alternatively, you could join the fragment to the preceding sentence:

✓   Being a skier who likes the sea, I enjoy living in Vancouver.

✓   I enjoy living in Vancouver, since I am a skier who likes the sea.

Run-on sentences

A run-on sentence is one that continues beyond the point where it should have stopped:

✗   Mosquitoes and blackflies are annoying, but they don't stop tourists from coming to spend their holidays in Canada and such is the case in Ontario's northland.

The *and* should be dropped and a period or semicolon added after *Canada*.

Another kind of run-on sentence is one in which two independent clauses are wrongly joined by a comma. An independent clause is a phrase that can stand by itself—a complete sentence. It shouldn't be attached to another sentence by a comma, unless a coordinating conjuction (joining word) is part of the link-up.

Northrop Frye won international acclaim as a critic, he was an English professor at the University of Toronto.

This error is known as a *comma splice* or a *fused sentence*. There are three ways of correcting it:

- by putting a period after *critic* and starting a new sentence:

    . . . as a critic. He . . .

- by replacing the comma with a semicolon:

    . . . as a critic; he . . .

- by making one of the independent clauses subordinate to the other, so that it can't stand by itself:

    Northrop Frye, who won international acclaim as a critic, was an English professor at the University of Toronto.

The one exception to the rule that independent clauses cannot be joined by a comma arises when the clauses are very short and arranged in a tight sequence:

✓   I opened the door, I saw the skunk, I shut the door.

Such instances are obviously uncommon.

Contrary to what many people think, words such as *however*, *therefore*, and *thus* cannot be used to join independent clauses:

✗   Two of my friends started out in Commerce, however they quickly decided they didn't like accounting.

This mistake can be corrected by beginning a new sentence after *Commerce* or (preferably) by putting a semicolon in the same place:

✓   Two of my friends started out in commerce; however, they quickly decided they didn't like accounting.

The only words that can be used to join independent clauses are the coordinating conjunctions—*and, or, nor, but, for, yet*, and *so*—and subordinating conjunctions such as *if, because, since, while, when, where, after, before*, and *until*. (See page 106 for more on the comma splice.)

Faulty predication

When the subject of a sentence is not grammatically connected to what follows (the predicate), the result is *faulty predication*:

✗   The <u>reason</u> he was defeated was <u>because</u> he couldn't handle people.

A sentence beginning with "The reason was" demands a "that" clause to complete it; the conjunction *because*—which means the same thing as *the reason was*—is redundant.

✓   The reason he was defeated was <u>that</u> he couldn't handle people.

Another solution is to rephrase the sentence:

✓   He was defeated because he couldn't handle people.

Faulty predication also occurs with *is when* and *is where* constructions:

✗   The climax <u>is when</u> the servant discovers the body.

Again, you can correct this error in one of two ways:
1. Follow the *is* with a noun phrase to complete the sentence.

✓   The climax is <u>the discovery of the body</u> by the servant.

(or)

✓   The climax is <u>the servant's discovery</u> of the body.

2. Change the verb:

✓ The climax <u>occurs</u> when the servant discovers the body.

Troubles with subject-verb agreement

Identifying the subject

A verb should always agree in number with its subject. Sometimes, however, when the subject does not come at the beginning of the sentence, or when it is separated from the verb by other information, you may be tempted to use a verb form that does not agree:

✗ The <u>increase</u> in the rate for freight and passengers <u>were condemned</u> by the farmers.

The subject here is *increase*, not *freight and passengers*; therefore the verb should be the singular *was condemned*:

✓ The <u>increase</u> in the rate for freight and passengers <u>was condemned</u> by the farmers.

Either, neither, each

The indefinite pronouns *either*, *neither*, and *each* always take singular verbs:

✗ <u>Neither</u> of the changing rooms <u>have</u> a sauna.

✓ <u>Each</u> of them <u>has</u> a shower.

Compound subjects

When *or*, *either . . . or*, or *neither . . . nor* is used to create a compound subject, the verb should usually agree with the last item in the subject:

✓ Neither my room-mate nor my <u>team-mates are going</u> home for the holiday.

If a singular item follows a plural item, however, a singular verb may sound awkward, and it's better to rephrase the sentence:

orig. Either my history <u>books</u> or my biology <u>text is going</u> to gather dust this weekend.

rev. This weekend, I'm going to leave behind either my history books or my biology text.

Unlike the word *and*, which creates a compound subject and therefore takes a plural verb, *as well as* or *in addition to* does not create a compound subject; therefore the verb remains singular:

✓ Tourtière <u>and</u> sugar-pie <u>are</u> traditional Quebec dishes.

✓ Tourtière <u>as well as</u> sugar-pie <u>is</u> a traditional Quebec dish.

Collective nouns

A collective noun is a singular noun, such as *family*, *army*, or *team*, that includes a number of members. If the noun refers to the members as one unit, it takes a singular verb:

✓ The <u>family goes</u> on holiday in June.

On the other hand, if the noun refers to the members as individuals, the verb becomes plural:

✓ The <u>team are receiving</u> their sweaters before the exhibition game.

✓ The <u>majority</u> of immigrants to Canada <u>settle</u> in cities.

Titles

A title is singular even if it contains plural words; therefore it takes a singular verb:

✓ <u>Tales of the South Pacific</u> was a best-seller.

✓ Goodman & Goodman is handling the legal dispute.

Tense troubles

Native speakers of English usually know the correct sequence of verb tense by ear, but a few tenses can still be confusing.

The past perfect

If the main verb is in the past tense and you want to refer to something before that time, use the past perfect (*had* plus the past participle). The time sequence will not be clear if you use the simple past in both clauses:

✗ He hoped that she <u>bought</u> the typewriter.

✓ He hoped that she <u>had bought</u> the typewriter.

Similarly, when you are reporting what someone said in the past — that is, when you are using past indirect discourse — you should use the past perfect tense in the clause describing what was said:

✗ He said that the party <u>caused</u> the neighbours to complain.

✓ He said that the party <u>had caused</u> the neighbours to complain.

Using ''if''

When you are describing a possibility in the future, use the present tense in the condition (*if*) clause and the future tense in the consequence clause:

✓   If he <u>tests</u> us on French verbs, I <u>will fail</u>.

When the possibility is unlikely, it is conventional—especially in formal writing—to use the subjunctive in the *if* clause, and *would* plus the base verb in the consequence clause:

✓   If he <u>were to cancel</u> the test, I <u>would cheer</u>.

When you are describing a hypothetical instance in the past, use the past subjunctive (it has the same form as the past perfect) in the *if* clause and *would have* plus the past participle for the consequence. A common error is to use *would have* in both clauses:

✗   If she <u>would have been</u> more friendly, I <u>would have asked</u> her to dance.

✓   If she <u>had been</u> more friendly, I <u>would have asked</u> her to dance.

Writing about literature

When you are describing a literary work in its historical context, use the past tense:

✓   Margaret Atwood <u>wrote</u> <u>Surfacing</u> at a time when George Grant's <u>Technology and Empire</u> <u>was persuading</u> people to reassess technocratic values.

To discuss what goes on *within* a work of literature, however, you should use the present tense:

✓   The narrator <u>retreats</u> to the woods and <u>tries</u> to escape the rationalism of her father's world.

When you are discussing an episode or incident in a literary work and want to refer to a prior incident or a future one, use past or future tenses accordingly:

✓   The narrator returns to northern Quebec, where she <u>spent</u> her summers as a child; by the time she leaves, she <u>will have rediscovered</u> herself.

Be sure to return to the present tense when you have finished referring to events in the past or future.

Pronoun troubles

Pronoun reference

The link between a pronoun and the noun it refers to must be clear. If the noun doesn't appear in the same sentence as the pronoun, it should appear in the preceding sentence:

✗ The textbook supply in the bookstore had run out, and so we borrowed them from the library.

Since *textbook* is used as an adjective rather than a noun, it cannot serve as referent or antecedent for the pronoun *them*. You must either replace *them* or change the phrase *textbook supply*:

✓ The textbook supply in the bookstore had run out, and so we borrowed the texts from the library.

✓ The textbooks in the bookstore had run out, and so we borrowed them from the library.

When a sentence contains more than one noun, make sure there is no ambiguity about which noun the pronoun refers to:

✗ The public wants increased social services along with lower taxes, but the government does not advocate them.

What does the pronoun *them* refer to? The taxes, the social services, or both?

✓ The public wants increased social services along with lower taxes, but the government does not advocate spending increases.

Using "it" and "this"

Using *it* and *this* without a clear referent can lead to confusion:

✗ Although the directors wanted to meet in January, it (this) didn't take place until May.

✓ Although the directors wanted to meet in January, the conference didn't take place until May.

Make sure that *it* or *this* clearly refers to a specific noun or pronoun.

Pronoun agreement — and sex

A pronoun should agree in number, person, and gender with the noun that it refers to:

✓ A working mother is fortunate if her workplace has a day-care centre for her young children.

Problems arise, however, when gender is not specified:

X When a Canadian civil <u>servant</u> retires, <u>their</u> pension is indexed.

This last error is becoming increasingly common because many writers, especially in North America, are reluctant to use the traditional "he" to refer to both sexes. Some language experts still say that this pronoun has a dual meaning, one for an individual male and one for any human. Others, with growing popular opinion on their side, maintain that the traditional usage is sexist.

There's no easy answer that will satisfy both sides in this dispute. On the one hand, it's sensible to avoid using language that may offend many as sexist. On the other hand, constant repetition of "he or she" and "his or her" is intrusive and awkward. Probably the most acceptable solution for now is to try to change the singular noun to the plural:

√ When Canadian civil <u>servants</u> retire, <u>their pensions</u> are indexed.

You can also use the occasional "he or she," as this book does. Whatever form you choose, check for agreement. Although conventions change, it is still a mistake to mix a singular noun with a plural pronoun:

X A leader must take responsibility for their action.

At least make it clear in your examples and illustrations that you are referring to females as well as males. In addition, use neutral nouns whenever possible—for examples, *sales agent* rather than *salesman*, or *flight attendant* rather than *stewardess*.

Using "one"
People often use the word *one* to avoid over-using *I* in their writing. Although in Britain this is common, in Canada and the United States frequent use of *one* may seem too formal and even a bit pompous:

If <u>one</u> were to apply for the grant, <u>one</u> would find oneself engulfed in so many bureaucratic forms that <u>one's</u> patience would be stretched thin.

Use *one* sparingly, and don't be afraid of the occasional *I*. The one error to avoid is mixing the third-person *one* with the second-person *you*:

X When <u>one</u> visits the Rockies, <u>you</u> are impressed by the grandeur of the scenery.

Using "me" and other objective pronouns
Remembering that it's wrong to say "Jane and me were invited to the

party," rather than "Jane and I were invited," many people use the subjective form of the pronoun even when it should be objective:

X He invited Jane and I to the party.

√ He invited Jane and me to the party.

The verb *invited* required an object, and *me* is the objective case. Here's a simple hint: read the sentence with only the problem pronoun. You will know by ear which form is correct:

He invited me to the party.

In most cases, prepositions should also be followed by the objective case (but see "Exceptions" below):

X Between you and I, Brown is a bore.

√ Between you and me, Brown is a bore.

X Eating well is a problem for we students.

√ Eating well is a problem for us students.

There are times, however, when the correct case can sound stiff or awkward:

orig. To whom was the award given?

Rather than keep to a correct but awkward form, try to reword the sentence:

rev. Who received the award?

Exceptions for pronouns following prepositions

The rule that a pronoun following a preposition takes the objective case has exceptions. When the preposition is followed by a clause, the pronoun should take the case required by its position in the clause:

X The Chairman showed some concern over whom would be selected as Dean.

Although the pronoun follows the preposition *over*, it is also the subject of the verb *would be selected* and therefore requires the subjective case:

√ The Chairman showed some concern over who would be selected as Dean.

Similarly, when a gerund (a word that acts partly as a noun and partly as a verb) is the subject of a clause, the pronoun that modifies it takes the possessive case:

X   Mother was elated by <u>him marrying</u> the Mayor's daughter.

√   Mother was elated by <u>his marrying</u> the Mayor's daughter.

X   He was tired of <u>me reminding</u> him.

√   He was tired of <u>my reminding</u> him.

Troubles with modifiers

Adjectives modify nouns; adverbs modify verbs, adjectives, and other adverbs. Do not use an adjective to modify a verb:

X   He played <u>good</u>. (Adjective with verb)

√   He played <u>well</u>. (Adverb modifying verb)

√   He played <u>really well</u>. (Adverb modifying adverb)

√   He had a <u>good style</u>. (Adjective modifying noun)

√   He had a <u>really good</u> style. (Adverb modifying adjective)

Squinting modifiers

Remember that clarity largely depends on word order: to avoid confusion, the relations between the different parts of a sentence must be clear. Modifiers should therefore be as close as possible to the words they modify. A *squinting modifier* is one that, because of its position, seems to look in two directions at once:

X   She expected <u>after the announcement</u> a decline in the stock market.

Was *after the announcement* the time of expectation or the time of the market decline? Changing the order of the sentence or rephrasing it will make the meaning clearer:

√   <u>After the announcement</u> she <u>expected</u> a decline in the stock market.

√   She expected the stock market to decline <u>after the announcement</u>.

Other squinting modifiers can be corrected in the same way:

X   Our English professor gave a lecture on <u>Beowulf, which was well illustrated</u>.

√   Our English professor gave a <u>well-illustrated lecture</u> on <u>Beowulf</u>.

Often the modifier works best when placed immediately in front of the phrase it modifies. Notice the difference that this placement can make:

> Only she guessed the motive for the theft.
> She only guessed the motive for the theft.
> She guessed only the motive for the theft.

Dangling modifiers

Modifiers that have no grammatical connection with anything else in the sentence are said to be *dangling*:

  ✗ Walking around the campus in June, the river and trees made a picturesque scene.

Who is doing the walking? Here's another example:

  ✗ <u>Reflecting</u> on the results of the referendum, it was decided not to press for independence for a while.

Who is doing the reflecting? Clarify the meaning by connecting the dangling modifier to a new subject:

  ✓ <u>Walking</u> around the campus in June, <u>she</u> thought the river and trees made a picturesque scene.

  ✓ <u>Reflecting</u> on the results of the referendum, <u>they</u> decided not to press for independence for a while.

Troubles with pairs and parallels

Comparisons

Make sure that your comparisons are complete. The second element in a comparison should be equivalent to the first, whether the equivalence is stated or merely implied:

  ✗ Today's students have a greater understanding of calculus than their parents.

This sentence suggests that the two things being compared are *calculus* and *parents*. Adding a second verb (*have*) equivalent to the first one shows that the two things being compared are *parents' understanding* and *students' understanding*:

  ✓ Today's students <u>have</u> a greater understanding of calculus than their parents <u>have</u>.

A similar problem arises in the following comparison:

  ✗ That cabinet minister is <u>a tiresome man</u> and so are his press conferences.

Press conferences may be tiresome, but they are not *a tiresome man*; to make sense, the two parts of the comparison must be parallel:

  ✓ That cabinet minister is <u>tiresome</u>, and so are his press conferences.

Correlatives (coordinate constructions)

Constructions such as *both . . . and, not only . . . but,* and *neither . . . nor* are especially tricky. The coordinating term must not come too early, or else one of the parts that come after will not connect with the common element. For the implied comparison to work, the two parts that come after the coordinating term must be grammatically equivalent:

X   He not only bakes cakes but bread.

✓   He bakes not only cakes but bread.

Parallel phrasing

A series of items in a sentence should be phrased in parallel wording. Make sure that all the parts of a parallel construction are in fact equal:

X   Mackenzie King loved his job, his dogs, and mother.

✓   Mackenzie King loved his job, his dogs, and his mother.

Once you have decided to include the pronoun *his* in the first two elements, the third must have it too.

For clarity as well as stylistic grace, keep similar ideas in similar form:

X   He failed Economics and barely passed Statistics, but Political Science was a subject he did well in.

✓   He failed Economics and barely passed Statistics, but did well in Political Science.

11

Punctuation

Punctuation causes students so many problems that it deserves a chapter of its own. If your punctuation is faulty, your readers will be confused and may have to backtrack; worse still, they may be tempted to skip over the rough spots. Punctuation marks are the traffic signals of writing; use them with precision to keep readers moving smoothly through your work.

Period [.]

1. Use a period at the end of a sentence.   A period indicates a full stop, not just a pause.

2. Use a period with abbreviations.   British style omits the period in certain cases, but North American style usually requires it for abbreviated titles (Mrs., Dr., etc.) as well as place-names (B.C., N.W.T., etc.). Although the abbreviations and acronyms for some organizations include periods, the most common ones generally do not (CARE, CIDA, etc.).

3. Use a period at the end of an indirect question.   Do *not* use a question mark:

   X He asked if I wanted a substitute?

   √ He asked if I wanted a substitute.

   X I wonder where she went?

   √ I wonder where she went.

4. Use a period for questions that are really polite orders:

√ Will you please send him the report by Friday.

Comma [,]

Commas are the trickiest of all punctuation marks: even the experts differ on when to use them. Most agree, however, that too many commas are as bad as too few, since they make writing choppy and awkward to read. Certainly recent writers use fewer commas than earlier stylists did. Whenever you are in doubt, let clarity be your guide. The most widely accepted conventions are these:

1. Use a comma to separate two independent clauses joined by a coordinating conjunction (and, but, for, or, nor, yet, so). By signalling that there are two clauses, the comma will prevent the reader from confusing the beginning of the second clause with the end of the first:

X He went out for dinner with his sister and his room-mate joined them later.

√ He went out for dinner with his sister, and his room-mate joined them later.

When the second clause has the same subject as the first, you have the option of omitting both the second subject and the comma:

√ He can stick-handle well, but he can't shoot.

√ He can stick-handle well but can't shoot.

If you mistakenly punctuate two sentences as if they were one, the result will be a *run-on sentence*; if you use a comma but forget the coordinating conjunction, the result will be a *comma splice*:

X He took his family to the zoo, it was closed for repairs.

√ He took his family to the zoo, but it was closed for repairs.

Remember that words such as *however, therefore,* and *thus* are *conjunctive adverbs*, not conjunctions: if you use one of them to join two independent clauses, the result will again be a *comma splice*:

X She was accepted into medical school, however, she took a year off to earn her tuition.

√ She was accepted into medical school; however, she took a year off to earn her tuition.

Conjunctive adverbs are often confused with conjunctions. You can distinguish between the two if you remember that a conjunctive adverb's position in a sentence can be changed:

✓ She was accepted into medical school; she took a year off, <u>however,</u> to earn her tuition.

The position of a conjunction, on the other hand, is invariable; it must be placed between the two clauses:

✓ She was accepted into medical school, <u>but</u> she took a year off to earn her tuition.

A good rule of thumb, then, is to *use a comma when the linking word can't move.*

When, in rare cases, the independent clauses are short and closely related, they may be joined by a comma alone:

✓ I came, I saw, I conquered.

2. Use a comma between items in a series   (place a coordinating conjunction before the last item):

✓ She finally found an apartment that was large, bright, and clean.

✓ Then she had to scrounge around for dishes, pots, cutlery, and a kettle.

The comma before the conjunction is optional:

✓ She kept a cat, a dog and a budgie.

Sometimes, though, the final comma can help to prevent confusion:

✓ When we set off on our trip, we were warned about passport thieves, attacks on single women, and lost children.

In this case, the comma prevents the reader from thinking that *attacks* are made on lost children as well as *single women.*

3. Use a comma to separate adjectives preceding a noun when they modify the same element:

✓ It was a rainy, windy night.

When the adjectives *do not* modify the same element, however, you should not use a comma:

✓ It was a pleasant winter outing.

Here *winter* modifies *outing*, but *pleasant* modifies the total phrase *winter outing*. A good way of checking whether or not you need a comma is to see if you can reverse the order of the adjectives. If you can reverse it (*rainy, windy night* or *windy, rainy night*), use a comma; if you can't (*winter pleasant outing*), omit the comma.

4. Use commas to set off an interruption (an interrupting word or phrase is technically called a parenthetical element):

✓ The film, I hear, isn't nearly as good as the book.

✓ My tutor, however, couldn't answer the question.

Remember to put commas on *both sides* of the interruption:

✗ The music, they say was adapted from a piece by Mozart.

✓ The music, they say, was adapted from a piece by Mozart.

5. Use commas to set off words or phrases that provide additional but non-essential information:

✓ Our president, Sue Stephens, does her job well.

✓ The black retriever, his closest companion, went with him everywhere.

Sue Stephens and *his closest companion* are *appositives*: they give additional information about the nouns they refer to (*president* and *retriever*), but the sentences would be understandable without them. Here's another example:

✓ My oldest friend, who lives in Halifax, was married last week.

The phrase *who lives in Halifax* is a *non-restrictive* modifier, because it does not limit the meaning of the word it modifies (*friend*). Without that modifying clause the sentence would still specify who was married. Since the information the clause provides is not necessary to the meaning of the sentence, you must use commas on both sides to set it off.

In contrast, a *restrictive* modifier is one that provides essential information; therefore it must not be set apart from the element it modifies, and commas should not be used:

✓ The man who came to dinner was my uncle.

Without the clause *who came to dinner*, the reader would not know which man was the uncle.

To avoid confusion, be sure to distinguish carefully between essential and additional information. The difference can be important:

Students, who are unwilling to work, should not receive grants.

Students who are unwilling to work should not receive grants.

6. Use a comma after an introductory phrase when omitting it would cause confusion:

X On the balcony above the singers entertained the diners.

√ On the balcony above, the singers entertained the diners.

X When he turned away the prisoner disappeared.

√ When he turned away, the prisoner disappeared.

7. Use a comma to separate elements in dates and addresses:

February 2, 1993. (Commas are often omitted if the date comes first: 2 February 1993.)

117 Hudson Drive, Edmonton, Alberta.

They lived in Dartmouth, Nova Scotia.

8. Use a comma before a quotation in a sentence:

He said, "Life is too short to worry."

"The children's safety," he warned, "is in your hands."

For more formality, or if the part preceding the quotation is a complete sentence, use a colon (see p. 110).

9. Use a comma with a name followed by a title:

David Gunn, President
Alice Smith, M.D.

Semicolon [;]

1. Use a semicolon to join independent clauses (complete sentences) that are closely related:

For five days he worked non-stop; by Saturday he was exhausted.

His lecture was confusing; no one could understand the terminology.

A semicolon is especially useful when the second independent clause begins with a conjunctive adverb such as *however, moreover, conse-*

quently, nevertheless, in addition, or *therefore* (usually followed by a comma):

> He ate a whole bag of doughnuts; consequently, he felt sick in class.

Some grammarians may disagree, but it's usually acceptable to follow a semicolon with a coordinating conjunction if the second clause is complicated by other commas:

> John, my cousin, is a keen jogger in all weather; but sometimes, especially in winter, I think it does him more harm than good.

2. Use a semicolon to mark the divisions in a complicated series when individual items themselves need commas. Using a comma to mark the subdivisions and a semicolon to mark the main divisions will help to prevent mix-ups:

> X He invited Prof. Brooks, the vice-principal, Jane Hunter, and John Taylor.

Is the vice-principal a separate person?

> √ He invited Prof. Brooks, the vice-principal; Jane Hunter; and John Taylor.

In a case such as this, the elements separated by the semicolon need not be independent clauses.

Colon [:]

A colon indicates that something is to follow.

1. Use a colon before a formal statement or series:

> The winners are the following: Anna, George, and Hugh.

Do not use a colon if the words preceding it do not form a complete sentence:

> X The winners are: Anna, George, and Hugh.
> √ The winners are Anna, George, and Hugh.

On the other hand, a colon often precedes a vertical list, even when the introductory part is not a complete sentence:

> √ The winners are: Anna Singh
>   George Turner
>   Hugh Mackay

2. Use a colon for formality before a direct quotation, or when a complete sentence precedes the quotation:

> The leaders of the anti-nuclear group repeated their message: "The world needs bread before bombs."

Dash [—]

A dash creates an abrupt pause, emphasizing the words that follow. (Never use dashes as casual substitutes for other punctuation: overuse can detract from the calm, well-reasoned effect you want.)

1. Use a dash to stress a word or phrase:

> The British—as a matter of honour—vowed to retake the islands.
>
> Foster was well received in the legislature—at first.

2. Use a dash in interrupted or unfinished dialogue:

> "It's a matter—to put it delicately—of personal hygiene."

In typing, use two hyphens together, with no spaces on either side, to show a dash.

Exclamation mark [!]

An exclamation mark helps to show emotion or feeling. It is usually found in dialogue:

> "Woe is me!" she mourned.

In academic writing, you should use it only in those rare cases when you want to give a point an emotional emphasis:

> He concluded that the economic downturn would be short-lived. Some forecast!

Quotation marks [" " or ' ']

Quotation marks are usually double in American style and single in British. In Canada either is accepted—just be consistent.

1. Use quotation marks to signify direct discourse (the actual words of a speaker):

> I asked, "What is the matter?"
> He said, "I have a pain in my big toe."

2. Use quotation marks to show that words themselves are the issue:

> The term "love" in tennis comes from the French word for "egg."

Alternatively, you may italicize or underline the terms in question.

Sometimes quotation marks are used to mark a slang word or an inappropriate usage, to show that the writer is aware of the difficulty:

> Hitler's "final solution" was the most barbaric act of this century.

Use this device only when necessary; usually it's better to let the context show your attitude, or to choose another term.

3. Use quotation marks to enclose the titles of poems, short stories, songs, films, and articles in books or journals. In contrast, titles of books, paintings, or music are italicized or underlined:

> The story I like best in Robert Weaver's <u>Canadian Short Stories</u> is "Bernadette" by Mavis Gallant.

4. Use quotation marks to enclose quotations within quotations (single or double depending on your primary style):

> He said, "Hitler's 'final solution' was the most barbaric act of this century."

Placement of punctuation with quotation marks

Both British and the American practices are accepted in Canada. British style usually places the punctuation outside the quotation marks, unless it is actually part of the quotation. The American practice, followed in this book, is increasingly common in Canada:

• A comma or period always goes inside the quotation marks:

> He said, "Give me another chance," but I replied, "You've had enough chances."

• A semicolon or colon always goes outside the quotation marks:

George wants to watch "Kids in the Hall"; I'd rather watch the hockey game.

- A question mark, dash, or exclamation mark goes inside quotation marks if it is part of the quotation, but outside if it is not:

He asked, "What is for dinner?"

Did he really call the boss a "lily-livered hypocrite"?

His speech was hardly an appeal for "blood, sweat and tears"!

I was just whispering to Mary, "That instructor is a—" when suddenly he glanced at me.

- When a reference is given parenthetically (in round brackets) at the end of a quotation, the quotation marks precede the parentheses and the sentence punctuation follows them:

Lipsey suggested that we should "abandon the Foreign Investment Review Agency" (Globe and Mail, 12 April 1983).

Apostrophe [']

The apostrophe forms the possessive case for nouns and some pronouns. (Remember that possession may also be shown without an apostrophe if the possession is linked instead by *of*: *the crux of the argument, the end of the day*. This form is usual for things rather than people.)

1. Add an apostrophe followed by "s" to

- all singular and plural nouns *not* ending in *s*: *cat's, women's*.
- singular *proper* nouns ending in *s*: *Keats's, Sis's* (but note that the final *s* can be omitted if the word has a number of them already and would sound awkward, as in *Jesus'* or classical names such as *Socrates'*).
- indefinite pronouns: *someone's, anybody's*, etc.

2. Add an apostrophe to plural nouns ending in "s": *families', houses', cars'*.

3. Use an apostrophe to show contractions of words: *isn't, can't, winter of '87*. Caution: don't confuse *it's* (the contraction of *it is*) with the possessive of *it — its —* which has no apostrophe.

Parentheses [( )]

1. Use parentheses to enclose an explanation, example, or qualification. Parentheses show that the enclosed material is of incidental importance to the main idea. They make a less pronounced interruption than a dash, but a more pronounced one than a comma:

> My wife (the eldest of five children) is a superb cook and carpenter.
>
> His latest plan (according to neighbours) is to dam the creek.

Remember that although punctuation should not precede parentheses, it may follow them if required by the sense of the sentence:

> I like coffee in the morning (if it's not instant), but she prefers tea.

If the parenthetical statement comes between two complete sentences, it should be punctuated as a sentence, with the period inside the parentheses:

> I finished my last essay on April 30. (It was on Aristotle's ethics.) Fortunately, I had three weeks free to study for the exam.

2. Use parentheses to enclose references. See Chapters 12 and 13 for details.

Brackets [ ]

Brackets are square enclosures, not to be confused with parentheses (which are round).

1. Use brackets to set off a remark of your own within a quotation. They show that the words enclosed are not those of the person quoted:

> Fox maintained, "Obstacles to western unification [in the eighties] are as many as they are serious."

Brackets are sometimes used to enclose *sic* (Latin for *thus*), which is used after an error, such as a misspelling, to show that the mistake was in the original. *Sic* should be underlined:

> The politician, in his letter to constituents, wrote about "these parlouse [sic] times of economic difficulty."

Hyphen [-]

1. Use a hyphen if you must divide a word at the end of a line. When a word is too long to fit at the end of a line, it's best to keep it in one piece by starting a new line. If you must divide, however, remember these rules:
- Divide between syllables.
- Never divide a one-syllable word.
- Never leave one letter by itself.
- Divide double consonants except when they come before a suffix, in which case divide before the suffix:

> ar-rangement
> embar-rassment
> fall-ing
> pass-able

When the second consonant has been added to form the suffix, keep it with the suffix:

> refer-ral
> begin-ning

2. Use a hyphen to separate the parts of certain compound words:

compound nouns:	sister-in-law, vice-consul
compound verbs:	test-drive, proof-read
compound adjectives:	well-considered plan, twentieth-century attitudes

Note that compound adjectives are hyphenated only when they *precede* the part modified. Otherwise, omit the hyphen:

> The plan was well considered.

> These are attitudes of the twentieth century.

After long-time use, some compound nouns drop the hyphen. When in doubt, check a dictionary.

3. Use a hyphen with certain prefixes (*all-, self-, ex-,* and those prefixes preceding a proper name):

> all-party, self-imposed, ex-jockey, anti-nuclear, pro-Canadian.

4. Use a hyphen to emphasize contrasting prefixes:

> The coach agreed to give both pre- and post-game interviews.

5. *Use a hyphen to separate written-out compound numbers from one to a hundred and compound fractions used as modifiers:*

> eighty-one years ago
> seven-tenths full

6. *Use a hyphen to separate parts of inclusive numbers or dates:*

> the years 1890-1914
> pages 3-40

Ellipsis [. . .]

1. Use an ellipsis to show an omission from a quotation:

> He reported that "the drought in the thirties, to many farming families in the west . . . resembled a biblical plague, even to the locusts."

If the omission comes at the end of a sentence, add the original period (without a space) before the ellipsis.

> According to Morris, his actions "were often misunderstood. . . . Only later did his motives become clear."

2. Use an ellipsis to show that a series of numbers continues indefinitely:

> 1, 3, 5, 7, 9 . . .

Italics [*italics*], underlining, or boldface

Italics are slanted (cursive) letters. If you use a typewriter that can't produce italics, underlining is an acceptable substitute. It is also becoming acceptable practice with word-processors to use boldface type in place of either, although italics are still most common.

1. Use italics for the titles of books, long poems that are complete books, plays, films, and lengthy musical pieces:

> Davies's <u>Fifth Business</u> is one of my favourite novels.

Note: for articles, essays, and short poems or musical pieces, use quotation marks. If the title contains another title, be sure to set it off in the correct style:

- When both titles are books (or book-length), use quotation marks for the internal one:

  Her latest book is A Post-Modern Reading of "Hamlet."

- When the internal title is a book but the main title is not, use italics (underlining):

  For more detail, see his recent article, "The Perception of Advertising in McLuhan's Understanding Media."

- When neither title is a book, use the alternate form of quotation marks:

  Her essay is entitled "Imagery in Keats's 'To Autumn.'"

2. Use italics to emphasize an idea:

  It is important that all equipment be washed immediately.

Be sparing with this use, interspersing it with other, less intrusive methods of creating emphasis.

3. Use italics (or quotation marks) to emphasize a word as a word:

  The term peer group is an example of sociological jargon.

4. Use italics for foreign words or expressions:

  The final sentence of her argument is a non sequitur.

Chapter

12

Documentation in

the humanities

This chapter is specifically intended as a guide for handling quotations, footnotes, and bibliographies in humanities subjects; however, it may also be useful for some subjects in the social sciences.

Quotations

Quotations can add authority to your writing as well as help you avoid charges of plagiarism. But you should use them with care: never quote a passage just because it sounds impressive. Be sure that it really adds to your discussion, either by expressing an idea with special force or cogency, or by giving substance to a debatable point.

Guidelines for incorporating quotations

1. Integrate the quotation so that it makes sense in the context of your discussion and fits grammatically into a sentence:

X Henry Ford had little knowledge of history. He proclaimed, "History is bunk," but his opinion is not one that many educated people would accept.

✓ Henry Ford had little knowledge of history. His opinion that "history is bunk" is not one that many educated people would accept.

2. Be accurate. Reproduce the exact wording, punctuation, and spelling of the original, including any errors. You can acknowledge a mistake by inserting the Latin word *sic* in square brackets after it (see p. 114). If you want to underline part of the quotation for emphasis, add *my emphasis* in brackets at the end.

3. Include as part of your text, enclosed in quotation marks,

• not more than four lines of prose;
• not more than three lines of verse. Use a slash (/) to indicate the end of a line:

> When Keats says, "That I may drink, and leave the world unseen/And with thee fade away into the forest dim," he is referring to the temptations of death.

4. Set off from your text by indenting (five to ten spaces) and omitting quotation marks
• five or more lines of prose;
• four or more lines of verse.

A long quotation is usually single-spaced and introduced by a colon. If the first line of your quotation is the first sentence of a new paragraph, indent the first line an extra three spaces:

> Machiavelli recognized the ability of a republic to change with the times:
>> Therefore, the truth is that a republic is of longer duration and has a much better fortune than a principality, for a republic, by virtue of its diverse citizenry, can better accommodate itself to the changeability of conditions than can a prince.

5. For a quotation within a quotation, use single quotation marks:

> A news report described the scene this way: "When the crowd heard de Gaulle shout, 'Vive le Québec libre!', they roared with approval."

6. If you want to omit something from the original, use ellipsis marks (three single-spaced periods):

> "The uprising was the result of indifference on the part of national leaders . . . and mismanagement on the part of civil servants."

If the omission is at the end of a sentence, add a fourth period.
To omit a full line of a poem, use a full line of single-spaced periods:

> Cedar and jagged fir
> . . . .
> against the gray
> and cloud-piled sky

7. If you want to insert an explanatory comment of your own into a quotation, enclose it in square brackets:

> "At private meetings, three western premiers [Harcourt, Romanow, and Filmon] strenuously objected to the federal proposal."

Note that brackets are square, not round; if your typewriter doesn't have a key for brackets, mark them by hand.

Traditional humanities documentation

This traditional approach uses both footnotes (or endnotes) and a bibliography. Many academic writers have abandoned it for the newer citation system, but it is still the preferred method for magazine articles, since it doesn't interrupt the flow of the text. Here is how it works.

Footnotes

Footnotes allow the reader to check sources and verify information. If you are quoting or summarizing other people's ideas, you also need them to avoid charges of plagiarism. But having too many notes can interrupt the reader's progress. To avoid clutter, remember that you don't need references to common knowledge or undisputed facts. As well, try to include in the text as much as you can of the footnote information, keeping the note itself as short as possible.

Use footnotes in four specific instances:
• to identify or document quotations;
• to acknowledge and give exact references to the words and ideas of others—even if you paraphrase or summarize them in your own words, rather than quote directly;
• to provide additional relevant information or comments that are difficult to fit into the text;
• to refer to other parts of a long discussion.

Format

1. For the reader's convenience, you may place your footnote at the bottom of the page on which the citation appears. Be sure to leave enough space; don't cram it into the margin at the bottom of the page. You should also leave a quadruple space between the text and the footnote, to make the division clear.

2. If you choose to place all your footnotes at the end of your writing you may call them *endnotes*. Using a separate page, underline your title—*Footnotes* or *Endnotes*—and centre the notes under it. Leave a triple space between the title and the first entry.

3. Whichever format you choose, remember to number your notes consecutively, using arabic numerals, and to put the corresponding number at the end of the sentence in which you make each reference, using superscript (a number slightly raised above the line of words). The numbers should follow all end punctuation. Traditionally, if you put footnotes at the bottom of the page, the numbering will begin again (1,2,3) with each page. Recently, though, writers have begun to number continuously from beginning to end of the text. With end-notes, the numbering is always continuous.

4. Bottom-of-the-page footnotes should be indented the same number of spaces that you use for a new paragraph. In student writing, they should be single-spaced, in contrast to the double-spaced text. Leave a double space between entries.

The following examples of documentation are restricted to the most common kinds of footnote and bibliographic references.

Footnotes for first references

Book by one author:

[1]Desmond Morton, Ministers and Generals: Politics and the Canadian Militia (Toronto: Univ. of Toronto Press, 1970), 20.

Capitalize the first letter in the title and subtitle, as well as the first letters of all words except for articles, prepositions, and conjunctions. If you give full bibliographic references later, you may omit subtitles in notes. Familiar terms such as *University* or *editor* may be abbreviated.

Book by two authors:

[2]Clara Thomas and John Lennox, William Arthur Deacon: A Canadian Literary Life (Toronto: Univ. of Toronto Press, 1982), 32.

Although the title page may list more than one place of publication (say, Toronto and Buffalo), you need name only the first place in your reference.

Book by three or more authors:

[3]Richard G. Lipsey et al., Economics, 4th ed. (New York: Harper and Row, 1982), 67.

Edition other than the first:

[4]Paul W. Fox, ed., Politics: Canada, 4th ed. (Toronto: McGraw-Hill Ryerson, 1977), 3.

Book with one editor:

> [5]Germaine Warkentin, ed., <u>Stories from Ontario: A Selection</u> (Toronto: Macmillan, 1974).

When the publisher's full title is lengthy, you may use its familiar short form; thus *Macmillan of Canada Ltd.* becomes simply *Macmillan.*

Book with two editors:

> [6]Ralph Krueger and Charles R. Bryfogle, eds., <u>Urban Problems</u> (Toronto: Holt, 1971).

Book by one author edited by another:

> [7]Hugh MacLennan, <u>The Other Side of Hugh MacLennan</u>, Elspeth Cameron, ed. (Toronto: Macmillan, 1978).

Book by one author translated by another:

> [8]<u>Plato's Republic</u>, G.M.A. Grube, trans. (Indianapolis: Huckett, 1974).

You need not list the author's name when it is part of the title.

Book in more than one volume:

> [9]Donald Creighton, <u>John A. Macdonald</u> (Toronto: Macmillan, 1955-56), 2 vols.

Article by one author in a work edited by another:

> [10]Michael Hornyansky, "Is Your English Destroying Your Image?" in <u>In the Name of Language</u>, Joseph Gold, ed. (Toronto: Macmillan, 1975).

Article in a journal with separate issues:

> [11]Jeffrey M. Heath, "The Private Language of Evelyn Waugh,' <u>English Studies in Canada</u> 2, no. 3 (Fall 1976), 329-39.

The abbreviations *p.* or *pp.* may be used to indicate page numbers, but increasingly they are omitted from references. Most page numbers may be contracted to avoid unnecessary repetition (for example, *33-7, 465-82, 1277-9*); however, numbers between *10* and *20* should always be written in full (*10-11, 12-15, 214-18, 1342-1480*). If the issue of the journal in which the article appears is one of several bound together to form a single volume with continuous page numbers, you may leave out the week or month of publication. Just give the volume number, year (in parentheses), and page numbers:

> [11]George Woodcock, "Anarchist Phases and Personalities," <u>Queen's Quarterly</u> 87 (1980), 82-97.

Unsigned article in an encyclopedia:

> ¹²Encyclopedia Britannica: Micropaedia, 1974 ed., s.v. "Riel, Louis".

When citing entries in dictionaries and other unsigned, alphabetically arranged reference books, it's best to use *s.v.* (*sub verbo*, "under the word") rather than the volume and page numbers.

When an entry is signed, list the author's name first.

Government document:

> ¹³Canada Dept. of Labour, Women's Bureau, Changing Patterns in Women's Employment (Ottawa: Queen's Printer, 1966), 70.

Proceedings:

> ¹⁴Canadian Institute of International Affairs, Proceedings of Lester B. Pearson Conference on Canada-United States Relationship (Niagara-on-the-Lake, Ont.: n.p., 1976), 32.

The abbreviation *n.p.* indicates that there is no publisher.

Book review:

> ¹⁵Grant Reuber, rev. of On Economics and Society by Harry G. Johnson, Queen's Quarterly 83, no. 1 (Spring 1976), 129-30.

Signed newspaper article:

> ¹⁶Robert Gibbens, "Quebec Government Reviews Equipment Purchasing Policy," Globe and Mail, Report on Business, 2 Dec. 1982, B3.

Unsigned newspaper article:

> ¹⁷"Financing System Called Damaging to National Growth," Globe and Mail, 14 July 1982, 4.

Footnotes for subsequent references

1. Subsequent footnote references should usually be brief, including only the author's name and the page number:

> Morton, 22.

2. Instead of putting subsequent references as footnotes, you may enclose them in parentheses and include them in the body of the text, before the final punctuation in the referring sentence:

> Educators can also be trendy; the charge may be fair that those who deplore a return to the basics are "suffering from delirium trendens" (Hornyansky, 93).

3. If you are citing more than one work by an author, add the title (it may be in shortened form) after the author's name:

(Frye: <u>Modern Century</u>, 42)

4. If you are repeatedly referring to a single primary source, in references after the first you may simple enclose the page numbers in parentheses. If you are discussing a drama, refer to the act, scene, and line; if discussing a poem, refer to the verse and/or line.

Bibliographies

A bibliography is an alphabetical list of both those works cited in an essay and those found useful in preparing it. Your instructor may not require a bibliography if you document your references fully in footnotes, but it's a good idea to provide one.

Format

The format for bibliographies differs slightly from that for footnotes:

1. Use a separate page at the end of your essay, with an underlined heading, *Bibliography*, centred on the page.

2. Single-space all entries, leaving a double space between entries and a triple space between the heading and the first entry. Do not indent entries.

3. Do not number entries, but *list them alphabetically* by the author's or editor's surname. If no author is given, begin with the first significant word in the title.

4. Begin each bibliographic entry at the margin and indent any subsequent line five spaces.

5. Separate the main divisions by periods (rather than the commas and parentheses used in footnotes).

Book:

Fox, Paul W., ed. <u>Politics: Canada</u>. 4th ed. Toronto: McGraw-Hill Ryerson, 1977.

Frye, Northrop. <u>Anatomy of Criticism: Four Essays</u>. Princeton: Princeton Univ. Press, 1957.

If you include more than one work by a particular author, place the entries in alphabetical order by title (not counting any initial articles).

Give the name in the first entry only. For subsequent entries, type ten hyphens and a period. Leave two spaces and give the next title:

Hood, Hugh. The Governor's Bridge Is Closed. Toronto: Oberon, 1973.

----------. A New Athens. Toronto: Oberon, 1977.

If there is more than one author or editor, use inverted order for the first name only and natural order for the rest:

Thomas, Clara and John Lennox. William Arthur Deacon: A Canadian Literary Life. (Toronto: Univ. of Toronto Press, 1982.

Article in a book:

Ward, Barbara. "The First International Nation." In Canada: A Guide to the Peaceable Kingdom, 45-9. William Kilbourn, ed. Toronto: Macmillan, 1970.

Article in a journal:

Heath, Jeffrey M. "The Private Language of Evelyn Waugh." English Studies in Canada 2, no. 3 (Fall 1976), 329-39.

New MLA system for the humanities

One of the most respected authorities on documentation, the Modern Language Association of America, has introduced a new system of documentation for the humanities. This system is closer to the one used in the sciences and social sciences. Rather than references in footnotes or endnotes, it uses parenthetical citations in the text that correspond to more detailed bibliographical entries at the end of the paper. The bibliography itself lists only those works cited.

Be careful when using this system. Since the bibliography includes only those works you mention in the text, you may inadvertently fail to give credit to works you have found helpful in preparing your paper. To avoid the danger of plagiarism, you must make an effort to cite in the text all the works that helped to shape your opinions.

Here is an outline of the new MLA system for the most common types of citation.

In the text:

1. Put in parentheses (round brackets) only the information needed to identify a source clearly—usually the author's (or editor's) last name and the page of the text referred to:

> This type of musical parody is often "conservative in impulse" (Hutcheon, 92).

Place the parentheses where there is a pause in the sentence (usually at the end).

2. If the author's name is already given in the text, put in parentheses only the place of the reference:

> Harris see the logic in Hegel's argument (72-4).

Variations

- If you are citing an entire work, try to include the author's (or editor's) name in the text rather than in parentheses:

> In A Theory of Parody, Linda Hutcheon examines a range of contemporary art forms.

- For literary works, it may sometimes be more appropriate to cite information other than the page number — for example, the chapter, act and scene, or stanza. Unless your instructor prefers otherwise, use arabic numbers for these place numbers. For well-known literary works that you are citing repeatedly, you can use abbreviated titles, such as *MND* for *A Midsummer Night's Dream*:

> This image of marriage is echoed in the later comedy (MND, 4.2).

- If the work has more than one author, give all the names or add *et al.* to the first name — and use the same form in the bibliography.

> The same argument was applied to the universities (Matthews and Steele, 50-62).

- If the work is listed by title, give the title or a shortened version of it.
- If the work has a corporate author (for example, Government of Ontario), give the name of the organization or a shortened form.
- If the citation follows a quotation, place the parentheses after any quotation marks but before the end punctuation:

> The result, some claim, is "cultural suicide" (Jones et al., 42-52).

- If you are citing two or more works by the same author, include the appropriate title with each citation.

In the bibliography:

1. List only those works you have cited in the text.

2. At the top centre of the page, put the underlined title *Bibliography* or *List of Works Cited*.

3. Use the same format and style as for the bibliography in the traditional humanities system (see pp. 124-5).

Footnotes

You do not need footnotes in the new MLA system. They are useful only if you want to explain something you have said in the text; in other words, they are notes on content.

Do not put vital information in a footnote. At the same time, try to avoid footnotes that are really just information dumps — repositories for bits of detail you don't know what else to do with.

When you do need footnotes, use the same format as in the traditional humanities system (see Format, pp. 120-1).

For a more comprehensive survey of documentation, whether you use the traditional humanities approach or the newer citation method, consult one of the following:

• *MLA Handbook for Writers of Research Papers*, 3rd ed. Ed. Joseph Garibaldi and Walter S. Achtert (New York: Modern Language Association of America, 1988).
• Kate Turabian, *A Manual for Writers of Term Papers, Theses, and Dissertations*, 5th ed. (Chicago: Univ. of Chicago Press, 1988).

13

Documentation in the sciences

Methods of documentation in the sciences may differ widely even within a single discipline: always check with your instructor or department to make sure you are following the preferred practice. If your subject is one of the social sciences not listed in this chapter, find out if your department follows one of the common scientific approaches outlined here or a system for the humanities. For most social siences not listed the APA method advocated for psychology is probably the best choice.

Documentation in scientific reports, whatever the differences in detail, always has similar basic features:

1. You use brief references (termed *citations*) in the text itself, rather than footnotes.

2. At the end of the text you provide a section entitled *References* or *Literature Cited*, which lists only those works *directly referred to* in the text; other works consulted are not listed. The rules regarding plagiarism are the same as for any other kind of academic writing: see pages 15-16 and 118.

This chapter outlines the two methods for documentation in the sciences—alphabetical listing and consecutive listing[1]—and shows the conventions usually followed in each discipline. It also recommends journals that you may use as models. When the models for a particular subject differ, choose one method and follow it consistently. For any social science disciplines not listed here, the APA model used in psychology is probably the best option.

Alphabetical listing

In the text

1. The citation should usually be placed at the end of the sentence in which you refer to the work, with the author's surname and the year of publication in parentheses:

> Biologists have recently analysed the vascular flora in the boreal forests south of James Bay (Carleton & Maycock, 1980).

2. When referring to a specific page or table, include the number:

> (Carleton & Maycock, 1980, p. 121).
> (Smith, 1982, Table 3).

3. If you have already given the author's name in the text itself, all you need to add is the year:

> The work of Thaler and Plowright (1980) supports this hypothesis.

4. When citing a work with two authors, give both names. Usually an ampersand (&) is used in the parentheses, whereas *and* is used to separate the names in the text itself:

> Newborn infants will orient better to high-frequency than low-frequency sounds (Morongiello & Clifton, 1984), although Levanthal and Lipset (1964) found that neonates did not differentiate small frequency differences.

5. When citing a work by more than two authors, give the name of the first only, followed by *et al.*:

> O'Day et al. investigated this autoinhibitor of zygote giant cell formation (1981).

6. If you cite more than one work within parentheses, list them as follows:
- put several works by different authors in alphabetical order, separating them with semicolons:

> (Forstner, 1991; Lee, 1989; Zavitz, 1984)

- for several papers by one author, list them chronologically:

> (Forstner, 1987, 1989, 1991)

- for several papers by one author in the same year, put a letter marker after each:

> (Forstner, 1992a, 1992b)

In the reference section

Although specific details vary depending on the subject (see the sample entries below), all subjects in the alphabetical group share some features of reference style in common. Here are the general guidelines:

1. List your references alphabetically by author, surname first, followed by initials; do not number them.

2. For a work with two or more authors, list all their names (in most cases, only the first author's name should be reversed; give the rest in natural order).

3. When citing more than one work by a particular author, list the entries in chronological order (the date should usually follow the author's name). For works published in the same year, add a letter marker to each date (1982a, 1982b, etc.) After the first entry, omit the author's name (type ten hyphens and a period, then leave two spaces and continue: see p. 125).

4. For references to journals, always include the volume, issue, and page numbers.

Sample entries for specific subjects

In addition to the basic guidelines listed above, be sure to note the special features for each discipline. For more details, see the journals suggested as models.

Anthropology.   Book titles are capitalized (for the rules, see p. 121) but not underlined. The date precedes the title and the place of publication precedes the publisher's name. Model: *Canadian Journal of Anthropology* or *American Anthropologist.*

Book:
  McHugh, T. 1972. The Time of the Buffalo. New York: Knopf.

Journal:
  Mohr, A. 1980. Wishram birth and obstetrics. Ethnology 19:42, 7-445.

Astronomy.   Book titles are capitalized (for the rules, see p. 121) and underlined. The date is placed in parentheses, as are the publisher's name and the place of publication. The titles of articles are omitted and those of journals abbreviated. Volume numbers are underlined. Model: *The Astronomical Journal.*

Book:

> Baade, W. (1983). The Evolution of Stars and Galaxies (Harvard Univ. Press, Cambridge, Mass.).

Journal:

> Smith, R.M., G.V. Bicknell, A.R. Hyland, and T.J. Jones (1983). Astrophys.J. 266, 69-72.

Biology. Book titles are capitalized (see p. 121) but not underlined. The publisher's name precedes the place of publication. Journal titles may be abbreviated; for the accepted form, see the *1976 Biosis List of Serials.* Model: *Canadian Journal of Botany* or *Canadian Journal of Zoology.*

Book:

> Radford, A.E., W.C. Dickinson, J.R. Massey, and C.R. Bell. 1974. Vascular Plant Systematics. Harper and Row, New York.

Journal:

> Ouchterlony, O. 1958. Diffusion-in-gel methods for immunological analysis. Prog. Allergy, 5:1-78.

Earth Sciences. Titles are not underlined. The publisher's name precedes the place of publication. Model: *Canadian Journal of Earth Sciences* or *Geographical Society of America Bulletin.*

Book:

> Chow, V.T. 1969. Handbook of applied hydrology. McGraw-Hill, New York.

Journal:

> Dell, C. 1963. A study of the mineralogical composition of sand in northern Ontario. Canadian Journal of Soil Science, 43, pp. 189-200.

Psychology. The titles of books and journals are underlined, as are the volume numbers of journals. All authors' names are reversed (surname before initials), even when there is more than one. The date of publication follows the title of the book or journal. For more details, see the *Publication Manual* of the American Psychological Association (2nd ed.).

Book:

> Craik, F.I.M., and Trehuk, S.E. Aging and cognition processes. New York: Plenum Press. 1983.

Journal:

> Moscovitch, M. Right-hemisphere language. Topics in Language Disorders, 1981, 1, 4.

Consecutive listing

In the text

Instead of giving publication details in the text itself, use consecutive numbers (slightly raised above the line) to direct the reader to the reference section at the end of the paper:

> These findings are supported by Becker and Poë.[3]

Use the same number for every subsequent reference to the same work.

In the reference section

1. Arrange the references in the same order as in the text and number them accordingly.

2. Abbreviate journal titles.

Sample entries

Chemistry.   Book titles are usually enclosed in quotation marks; article titles are omitted. The author's name is listed with the surname preceding the initials. For the correct abbreviations of journal titles, see *CASSI—Chemical Abstracts Service Source Index* (Columbus, Ohio: The American Chemical Society, 1980). Model: *Journal of the American Chemical Society*.

Book:

> 1. Hoffman, B.E.M. "Coal gasifiers." The Energon Co.: Laramie, Wyoming, 1981; 15-50.

Journal:

> 2. Still, I.W.J.; Kutney, G.W. J. Org. Chem. 1981, 46, 4911.

Physics.   Authors' names are listed in natural order. The titles of articles are omitted. For journal abbreviations, see *CASSI—Chemical Abstracts Service Source Index* (Columbus, Ohio: The American

Chemical Society, 1980). Model: *Canadian Journal of Physics*; or see the *Style Manual* of the American Institute of Physics.

Book:
> 1. P. Jones and J. Jackson (Editors). Elections in Fluids. Pergamon. London, 1981.

Journals:
> 2. D.J. Dunlop and M.B. Zinn. Can. J. Earth Sci., 17, 1275-1285 (1980).

Note

[1]This division is based on that in *Notes on the Preparation of Essays in the Arts and Sciences* (Peterborough, Ont.: The Self-Instruction Centre, Trent University, 1979).

Catchlist of misused

words and phrases

accept, except. Accept is a verb meaning to *receive affirmatively*; **except**, when used as a verb, means to *exclude*:

> I accept your offer.
> The teacher excepted him from the general punishment.

accompanied by, accompanied with. Use **accompanied by** for people; **accompanied with** for objects:

> He was accompanied by his wife.
> The brochure arrived, accompanied with a discount coupon.

advice, advise. Advice is a noun, **advise** a verb:

> He was advised to ignore the others' advice.

affect, effect. As a verb to **affect** means to *influence*; as a noun it's a technical psychological term. The verb to **effect** means to *bring about*. The noun means *result*. In most cases, you will be safe if you remember to use **affect** for the verb and **effect** for the noun:

> The eye drops affect his vision.
> The effect of higher government spending is higher inflation.

alright. Always spell as two words: **all right**.

alternately, alternatively. Use **alternately** when you mean *in turn*: use **alternatively** when you mean *providing a choice or alternative*.

> When she addressed the crowd, she turned alternately to her left and her right.
> Alternatively, we can choose the less expensive printer.

all together, altogether. All together means *in a group*; **altogether** is an adverb meaning *entirely*:

He was altogether certain that the children were all together.

allusion, illusion. An **allusion** is an indirect reference to something; an **illusion** is a false perception:

> The rock image is an allusion to the myth of Sisyphus.
> He thought he saw a sea monster, but it was an illusion.

alot. Write as two separate words: *a lot*.

among, between. Use **among** for three or more persons or objects, **between** for two:

> Between you and me, there's trouble among the team members.

amoral, immoral. Amoral means *non-moral* or outside the moral sphere; **immoral** means *wicked*:

> As an art critic, he was amoral in his judgements.
> That immoral performance should be restricted to adults.

amount, number. Use **amount** for money or non-countable quantities; use **number** for countable items:

> No amount of wealth or number of expensive possessions will make up for a lack of love.

anyways. Non-standard English: use *anyway*.

as, because. As is a weaker conjunction than **because** and may be confused with *when*:

> X As I was working, I ate at my desk.
> ✓ Because I was working, I ate at my desk.
> X He arrived as I was leaving.
> ✓ He arrived when I was leaving.

as to. A common feature of bureaucratese; replace it with a single-word preposition such as *about* or *on*:

> They were concerned as to the range of disagreement.
> They were concerned about the range of disagreement.

> They recorded his comments as to the treaty.
> They recorded his comments on the treaty.

bad, badly. Bad is an adjective meaning *not good*:

> The meat tastes bad.
> He felt bad about forgetting the dinner party.

Badly is an adverb meaning *not well*; when used with the verbs

want or **need**, it means *very much*:

> She thought he played the villain's part badly.
> I badly need a new suit.

beside, besides. Beside is a preposition meaning *next to*:

> She worked beside her assistant.

Besides has two uses: as a preposition it means *in addition to*; as a conjunctive adverb it means *moreover*:

> Besides recommending the changes, the consultants are
> implementing them.
> Besides, it was hot and we wanted to rest.

between. See **among**.

bring, take. One **brings** something to a closer place and **takes** it to a farther one.

can, may. Can means to *be able*; **may** means to *have permission*:

> Can you fix the lock?
> May I have another piece of cake?

In speech, **can** is used to cover both meanings: in formal writing, however, you should observe the distinction.

can't hardly. A faulty combination of the phrases **can't** and **can hardly**. Use one or the other of them instead:

> He can't swim.
> He can hardly swim.

capital, capitol. As a noun **capital** may refer to a seat of government, the top of a pillar, an upper-case letter, or accumulated wealth. **Capitol** refers only to a specific American—or ancient Roman—legislative building.

complement, compliment. The verb to **complement** means to *complete*; to **compliment** means to *praise*.

> His engineering skill complements the skills of the designers.
> I complimented her on her outstanding report.

comprise, include. Comprise refers to all the parts of something, whereas **include** refers to some of them. Avoid the phrase "is comprised of."

> My class comprises twenty men and eighteen women; for the first time, it includes four exchange students from China.

continual, continuous. Continual means *repeated over a period of time*; **continuous** means *constant* or *without interruption*:

> The strikes caused continual delays in building the road.
> In August, it rained continuously for five days.

could of. Incorrect, as are **might of**, **should of**, and **would of**. Replace **of** with *have*.

> ✗ He could of done it.
> ✓ He could have done it.
> ✓ They might have been there.
> ✓ I should have known.
> ✓ We would have left earlier.

council, counsel. Council is a noun meaning an *advisory* or *deliberative assembly*. **Counsel** as a noun means *advice* or *lawyer*; as a verb it means to *give advice*.

> The college council meets on Tuesday.
> We respect his counsel, since he's seldom wrong.
> As a camp counsellor, you may need to counsel parents as well as children.

criterion, criteria. A **criterion** is a standard for judging something. **Criteria** is the plural of **criterion** and thus requires a plural verb:

> These are my criteria for selecting the paintings.

data. The plural of *datum*, **data** is increasingly treated as a singular noun, but this usage is not yet acceptable in formal prose: use a plural verb.

different than. Incorrect. Use either **different from** (American usage) or **different to** (British).

disinterested, uninterested. Disinterested implies impartiality or neutrality; **uninterested** implies a lack of interest:

> As a disinterested observer, he was in a good position to judge the issue fairly.
> Uninterested in the proceedings, he yawned repeatedly.

due to. Although increasingly used to mean *because of*, **due** is an adjective and therefore needs to modify something:

> ✗ Due to his impatience, we lost the contract. [Due is dangling]
> ✓ The loss was due to his impatience.

farther, further. Farther refers to distance, **further** to extent:

He paddled <u>farther</u> than his friends.
He explained the plan <u>further</u>.

good, well. **Good** is an adjective, not an adverb. **Well** can be both: as an adverb, it means *effectively*; as an adjective, it means *healthy*:

The pear sauce tastes <u>good</u>.
She is a <u>good</u> golfer.
She plays golf <u>well</u>.
At last, he is <u>well</u> again after his long bout of flu.

hanged, hung. **Hanged** means *executed by hanging*. **Hung** means *suspended* or *clung to*:

He was <u>hanged</u> at dawn for the murder.
He <u>hung</u> the picture.
He <u>hung</u> to the boat when it capsized.

hopefully. Use **hopefully** as an adverb meaning *full of hope*:

She scanned the horizon <u>hopefully</u>, waiting for her friend's ship to appear.

In formal writing, using **hopefully** to mean *I hope* is still frowned upon, although increasingly common; it's better to use *I hope*:

X   <u>Hopefully</u> we'll make a bigger profit this year.
✓   <u>I hope</u> we'll make a bigger profit this year.

imply, infer. **Imply** refers to what a statement suggests; **infer** relates to the audience's interpretation:

His letter <u>implied</u> that he was lonely.
I <u>inferred</u> from his letter that he would welcome a visit.

irregardless. Redundant; use *regardless*.

its, it's. **Its** is a form of possessive pronoun; **it's** is a contraction of *it is*. Many people mistakenly put an apostrophe in **its** in order to show possession.

X   The cub wanted <u>it's</u> mother.
✓   The cub wanted <u>its</u> mother.
✓   <u>It's</u> time to leave.

lead, led. Unlike the verb *read*, which does not change its spelling to form the past tense, the verb **lead** changes both its pronunciation and its spelling:

The path <u>leads</u> through the forest.
Isabel <u>led</u> the way.

less, fewer. Use **less** for money and things that are not countable; use **fewer** for things that are:

>Now that he's earning <u>less</u> money he's going to <u>fewer</u> movies.

lie, lay. To **lie** means to *assume a horizontal position*; to **lay** means to *put down*. The changes of tense often cause confusion:

Present	*Past*	*Past participle*
lie	lay	lain
lay	laid	laid

Remember that a person who is tired should "lie down", not "lay down."

like, as. **Like** is a preposition, but it is often wrongly used as a conjunction. To join two independent clauses, use the conjunction **as**:

> X I want to progress <u>like</u> you have this year.
> ✓ I want to progress <u>as</u> you have this year.
> ✓ Prof. Dodd is <u>like</u> my old school principal.

literally. This means *exactly as stated*. It does not mean *figuratively*.

> X I'm literally suffocating in this stuffy room.
> ✓ Such a sustained loud noise can <u>literally</u> damage the ears.

media. The plural of **medium**. Do not use as a singular noun:

> The most effective <u>medium</u> for advertising is television.
> Of the three <u>media</u> available, television is the most effective.

might of. See **could of**.

momentarily. This word means *for a brief time*. When you mean *very soon*, use *presently*.

> X The game will resume <u>momentarily</u>.
> ✓ The game will resume <u>presently</u>.
> ✓ The speaker has been delayed <u>momentarily</u> but will <u>presently</u> appear.

myself, me. **Myself** is an intensifier of, not a substitute for, *I* or *me*:

> X He gave it to John and <u>myself</u>.
> ✓ He gave it to John and <u>me</u>.
> X Jane and <u>myself</u> are invited.
> ✓ Jane and <u>I</u> are invited.
> ✓ <u>Myself</u>, I would prefer a swivel chair.

nor, or. Use **nor** with **neither** and **or** by itself or with **either**:

He is neither overworked nor underfed.
The plant is either diseased or dried out.

nuclear. Note the spelling; often misprounced as "nucular."

off of. Remove the unnecessary **of**:

X The fence kept the children off of the premises.
✓ The fence kept the children off the premises.

phenomenon. A singular noun: the plural is **phenomena**.

principal, principle. As an adjective, **principal** means *main* or *most important*; a **principal** is the *head of a school*. A **principle** is a *law* or *controlling idea*:

Our principal aim is to reduce the deficit.
Our principal, Prof. Smart, retires next year.
We are defending the island as a matter of principle.

rational, rationale. Rational is an adjective meaning *logical* or *able to reason*. **Rationale** is a noun meaning *explanation*:

That was not a rational decision.
The president sent around a memo with a rationale for his proposal.

real, really. The adjective **real** should never be used as an adverb; use *really* instead:

✓ We had real maple syrup with our pancakes.
X It was real good.
✓ It was really good.

set, sit. To **sit** means to *rest on the buttocks*; to **set** means to *put* or *place*:

After standing so long, you'll want to sit down.
Please set the bowl on the table.

should of. See **could of**.

their, there. Their is the possessive form of the third-person plural pronoun. **There** is usually an adverb, meaning *at that place* or *at that point*; sometimes it is used as an expletive (an introductory word in a sentence):

They parked their bikes there.
There is no point in arguing with you.

thus. A conjunctive adverb (see pp. 106-7). Can be used to link an independent clause and a verbal phrase, but not two independent clauses:

✓ He hung up, thus ending the discussion.
✗ He hung up, thus he ended the discussion.
✓ He hung up; thus he ended the discussion.

to, too, two. To is a preposition, as well as part of the infinitive form of a verb:

We went to town in order to shop.

Too is an adjective showing degree (the soup is *too* hot) or an adverb meaning *moreover*. **Two** is the spelled version of the number 2.

while. To avoid misreading, use **while** only when you mean *at the same time that*. Do not use it as a substitute for *although, whereas,* or *but*:

✗ While he's getting fair marks, he'd like to do better.
✗ I headed for home, while she decided to stay.
✓ He fell asleep while he was reading.

-wise. Never use **-wise** as a suffix to form new words when you mean *with regard to*:

✗ Sales-wise, the company did better last year.
✓ With regard to sales, the company did better last year.

(or)

✓ The company's sales increased last year.

would have, would of. When people are describing a hypothetical instance in the past, they often mistakenly use **would have** in both the condition (*if*) clause and the consequence clause: see p. 98. For **would of**, see *could of*.

your, you're. Your is a pronominal adjective used to show possession; **you're** is a contraction of *you are*:

You're likely to miss your train.

Glossary

abstract
a summary accompanying a formal scientific report or paper, briefly outlining the contents.

abstract language
theoretical language removed from concrete particulars: e.g., *justice, goodness, truth* (cf. **concrete language**).

acronym
a word made up of the first letters of a group of words: e.g., *NATO* for *North Atlantic Treaty Organization.*

active voice
see **voice**.

adjective
a word that modifies or describes a noun or pronoun, hence a kind of noun marker: e.g., *red, beautiful, solemn*. An **adjectival phrase** or **adjectival clause** is a group of words modifying a noun or pronoun.

adverb
a word that modifies or qualifies a verb, adjective, or adverb, often answering a question such as *how? why? when?* or *where?*: e.g., *slowly, fortunately, early, abroad*. An **adverbial phrase** or **adverbial clause** is a group of words modifying a verb, adjective, or adverb: e.g., *by force, in revenge*. See also **conjunctive adverb**.

agreement
consistency in tense, number, or person between related parts of a sentence: e.g., between subject and verb, or noun and related pronoun.

ambiguity
vague or equivocal language; meaning that can be taken two ways.

antecedent (referent)
the noun for which a pronoun stands.

appositive
a word or phrase that identifies a preceding noun or pronoun: e.g., *Mrs. Jones,* **my aunt**, *is sick*. The second phrase is said to be *in apposition* to the first.

article
a word that precedes a noun and shows whether the noun is definite or indefinite; a kind of determiner or noun-marker.
Indefinite article: *a (an)*.
Definite article: *the*.

assertion
a positive statement or claim: e.g., *The Senate is irrelevant.*

auxiliary
a verb used in combination with another verb to create a verb phrase; a helping verb used to create certain tenses and emphases: e.g., *could, do, may, will, have.*

bibliography

(a) a list of works referred to or found useful in the preparation of an essay or report; **(b)** a reference book listing works available in a particular subject.

case

the inflected form of pronouns (see **inflection**). **Subjective case:** *I, we, she, it, they.* **Objective case:** *me, us, him, her, it, them.* **Possessive case:** *my, our, his, her, its, their.*

circumlocution

a roundabout or circuitous expression: e.g., *in a family way* for *pregnant*; *at this point in time* for *now*.

clause

a group of words containing a subject and predicate. An **independent clause** can stand by itself as a complete sentence: e.g., *I bought a hamburger.* A **subordinate** or **dependent clause** cannot stand by itself but must be connected to another clause: e.g., **Since I was hungry,** *I bought a hamburger.*

cliché

a trite or well-worn expression that has lost its impact through overuse: e.g., *slept like a log, sunny disposition, tried and true.*

collective noun

a noun that is singular in form but refers to a group: e.g., *family, team, jury.* It may take either a singular or a plural verb, depending on whether it refers to individual members or to the group as a whole.

comma splice

see **run-on sentence**.

complement

a completing word or phrase that usually follows a linking verb to form a **subjective complement**: e.g., (1) *He is* **my father**. (2) *That cigar smells* **terrible**. If the complement is an adjective it is some-

times called a **predicate adjective**. An **objective complement** completes the direct object rather than the subject: e.g., *We found him* **honest and trustworthy**.

complex sentence

a sentence containing a dependent clause as well as an independent one: e.g., *I bought the ring, although it was expensive.*

compound sentence

a sentence containing two or more independent clauses: e.g., *I saw the car wreck and I reported it.* A sentence is called **compound-complex** if it contains a dependent clause as well as two independent ones: e.g., *When the fog lifted, I saw the car wreck and I reported it.*

conclusion

the part of an essay in which the findings are pulled together or implications revealed so that the reader has a sense of closure or completion. In a business report the conclusion is sometimes placed at the front.

concrete language

specific language, giving particular details (often details of sense): e.g., *red, corduroy dress, three long-stemmed roses* (cf. **abstract language**).

conjunction

an uninflected word used to link words, phrases, or clauses. A **coordinating conjunction** (e.g., *and, or, but, for, yet*) links two equal parts of a sentence. A **subordinating conjunction**, placed at the beginning of a subordinate clause, shows the logical dependence of that clause on another: e.g., (1) **Although** *I am poor, I am happy.* (2) **While** *others slept, he studied.* **Correlative conjunctions** are pairs of coordinating conjunctions (see **correlatives**).

conjunctive adverb

a type of adverb that shows the logical relation between the phrase or clause that it modifies and a preceding one: e.g., (1) *I sent the letter; it never arrived,* **however**. (2) *The battery died;* **therefore** *the car wouldn't start.*

connotation
associative meaning; the range of suggestion called up by a certain word. Apparent synonyms, such as *poor* and *underprivileged*, may have different connotations (cf. **denotation**).

context
the text surrounding a particular passage that helps to establish its meaning.

contraction
a word formed by combining and shortening two words: e.g., *isn't, can't, we're.*

coordinate construction
see **correlatives**.

coordinating conjunction
see **conjunction**.

copula verb
see **linking verb**.

correlatives (coordinates)
pairs of coordinating conjunctions: e.g., *either/or, neither/nor, not only/but.*

dangling modifier
a modifying word or phrase (often a participial phrase) that is not grammatically connected to any part of the sentence: e.g., **Walking to school**, *the street was slippery.*

demonstrative pronoun
a pronoun that points out something: e.g., (1) **This** *is his reason.* (2) **That** *looks like my lost earring.* When used to modify a noun or pronoun, a demonstrative pronoun becomes a kind of **pronominal adjective**: e.g., *this hat, those people.*

denotation
the literal or dictionary meaning of word (cf. **connotation**).

diction
the choice of words with regard to their tone, degree of formality, or register. Formal diction is the language of orations and serious essays. The informal diction of everyday speech or conversational writing can, at its extreme, become slang.

discourse
talk, either oral or written. **Direct discourse** gives the actual words spoken or written: e.g., *Donne said,* **"No man is an island."** In writing, direct discourse is put in quotation marks. **Indirect discourse** gives the meaning of the speech rather that the actual words. In writing, indirect discourse is not put in quotation marks: e.g., *He said that no one exists in an island of isolation.*

ellipsis marks
three spaced periods indicating an omission from a quoted passage.

endnote
a footnote or citation placed at the end of an essay or report.

essay
a literary composition on any subject. Some essays are descriptive or narrative, but in an academic setting most are expository (explanatory) or argumentative.

expletive
a grammatically meaningless exclamation or phrase. The most common expletives are the sentence beginnings *It is* and *There is (are).*

exploratory writing
the informal writing done to help generate ideas before formal planning begins.

footnote
a citation placed at the bottom of a page or the end of the composition (cf. **endnote**).

fused sentence
see **run-on sentence**.

general language
language lacking specific details; abstract language.

gerund
a verbal (part-verb) that functions as a noun and is marked by an *-ing* ending: e.g., **Swimming** *can help you become fit.*

grammar
a study of the forms and relations of words, and of the rules governing their use in speech and writing.

hypothesis
a supposition or trial proposition made as a starting point for further investigation. The plural is *hypotheses.*

hypothetical instance
a supposed occurrence; often shown by a clause beginning with *if.*

indefinite article
a (an). Definite article: *the.*

independent clause
see **clause**.

indirect discourse
see **discourse**.

infinitive
a type of verbal not connected to any subject: e.g., *to ask.* The **base infinitive** omits the *to*: e.g., *ask.*

inflection
the change in the form of a word to indicate number, person, case, tense, or degree.

integrate
combine or blend together.

intensifier (qualifier)
a word that modifies and adds emphasis to another word or phrase: e.g., **very** *tired*, **quite** *happy*, *I* **myself**.

interjection
a remark or exclamation interposed or thrown into a speech, usually accompanied by an exclamation mark: e.g., *Oh dear! Alas!*

interrogative sentence
a sentence that asks a question: e.g., *What is the time?*

intransitive verb
a verb that does not take a direct object : e.g., *fall, sleep, talk.*

italics
slanting type used for emphasis, replaced in typescript by underlining.

jargon
technical terms used unnecessarily or in inappropriate places: e.g., *peer-group interaction* for *friendship*.

linking verb (copula verb)
the verb *to be* used to join subject to complement: e.g., *The apples* **were** *ripe.*

literal meaning
the primary, or denotative, meaning of a word.

logical indicator
a word or phrase – usually a conjunction or conjunctive adverb – that shows the logical relation between sentences or clauses: e.g., *since, furthermore, therefore.*

modifier
a word or group of words that describes or limits another element in the sentence. A **misplaced modifier** causes confusion because it is not placed next to the element it should modify: e.g., *I only ate the pie.* [Revised: *I ate only the pie.*]

mood
(a) as a grammatical term, the form that shows a verb's function (indicative, imperative, interrogative, or subjunctive); **(b)** when applied to literature generally, the state of mind or feeling shown.

non-restrictive element
see **restrictive element**.

noun
an inflected part of speech marking a person, place, thing, idea, action, or feeling, and usually serving as subject, object, or complement. A **common** noun is a general term: e.g., *dog, paper, automobile*. A **proper noun** is a specific name: e.g., *Mary, Sudbury, Skidoo.*

object
(a) a noun or pronoun that, when it completes the action of a verb, is called a **direct object**: e.g., *He passed the* **puck**. An **indirect object** is the person or thing receiving the direct object: e.g., *He passed the* **puck** (direct object) *to* **Richard** (indirect object). **(b)** The noun or pronoun in a group of words beginning with a preposition; pronouns take the objective case: e.g., *at the* house, *about* her, *for* me.

objective complement
see **complement**.

objectivity
a disinterested stance; a position taken without personal bias or prejudice (cf. **subjectivity**).

outline
with regard to an essay or report, a brief sketch of the main parts; a written plan.

paragraph
a unit of sentences arranged logically to explain or describe an idea, event, or object; usually marked by indentation of the first line.

parallel wording
wording in which a series of items has a similar grammatical form: e.g., *At her marriage my grandmother promised* **to love, to honour, and to obey** *her husband.*

paraphrase
restate in different words.

parentheses
curved lines, enclosing and setting off a passage; not to be confused with square brackets.

parenthetical element
an interrupting word or phrase: e.g., *My musical career,* **if it can be called that**, *consisted of playing the triangle in kindergarten.*

participle
a verbal (part-verb) that functions as an adjective. Participles can be either **present**, usually marked by an *-ing* ending (e.g. *taking*), or **past** (*having taken*); they can also be passive (*having been taken*).

parts of speech
the major classes of words. Some grammarians include only function words (nouns, verbs, adjectives, and adverbs); others also include pronouns, prepositions, conjunctions, and interjections.

passive voice
see **voice**.

past participle
see **participle**.

periodic sentence
a sentence in which the normal order is inverted or an essential element suspended until the very end: e.g., *Out of the house, past the grocery store, through the school yard and down the railroad tracks* **raced the frightened boy**.

person
in grammar, the three classes of personal pronouns referring to the person speaking (first person), person spoken to (second person), and person spoken about (third person). With verbs, only the third person singular has a distinctive form.

personal pronoun
see **pronoun**.

phrase
a unit of words lacking a subject-predicate combination. The most common

kind is the **prepositional phrase**--a unit comprising preposition plus object. Some modern grammarians also refer to the **single-word phrase**.

plural
indicating two or more in number. Nouns, pronouns, and verbs all have plural forms.

possessive case
see **case**.

prefix
a syllable placed in front of the root form of a word to make a new word: e.g., *pro-, in-, sub-* (cf. **suffix**).

preposition
a short word heading a unit of words containing an object, thus forming a **prepositional phrase**: e.g., **under** *the tree*, **before** *my time*.

pronoun
a word that stands in for a noun. A **personal pronoun** stands in for the name of a person: *I, he, she, we, they,* etc.

punctuation
a conventional system of signs used to indicate stops or divisions in a sentence and to make meaning clearer: e.g., comma, period, semicolon, etc.

reference works
material consulted when preparing an essay or report.

referent (antecedent)
the noun for which a pronoun stands.

register
the degree of formality in word choice and sentence structure.

relative clause
a clause headed by a relative pronoun: e.g. *the man* **who came to dinner** *is my uncle.*

relative pronoun
who, which, what, that, or their com-pounds beginning an adjective or noun clause: e.g., *the house* **that** *Jack built*; **whatever** *you say.*

restrictive element
a phrase or clause that identifies or is essential to the meaning of a term: e.g., *The book* **that I need** *is lost.* It should not be set off by commas. A non-restrictive element is not needed to identify the term and is usually set off by commas: e.g., *The book,* **which I got from my aunt**, *is one of my favourites.*

run-on sentence
a sentence that goes on beyond the point where it should have stopped. The term covers both the **comma splice** (two sentences joined by a comma) and the **fused sentence** (two sentences joined without any punctuation between them).

sentence
a grammatical unit that includes both a subject and a predicate. The end of a sentence is marked by a period.

sentence fragment
a group of words lacking either a subject or a verb; an incomplete sentence.

simple sentence
a sentence made up of only one clause: e.g., *Joan climbed the tree.*

slang
colloquial speech, not considered part of standard English; often used in a special sense by a particular group: e.g., *gross* for *disgusting*; *gig* as a musician's term.

split infinitive
a construction in which a word is placed between *to* and the base verb: e.g., *to completely finish*.

squinting modifier
a kind of misplaced modifier; one that could be connected to elements on either side, making meaning ambiguous: e.g., *When he wrote the letter* **finally** *his boss thanked him.*

standard English
the English currently spoken or written by literate people over a wide geographical area.

subject
in grammar, the noun or noun equivalent about which something is predicated; that part of a clause with which the verb agrees: e.g., **They** *swim every day when the* **pool** *is open.*

subjective complement
see **complement**.

subjectivity
a personal stance, not impartial (cf. **objectivity**).

subordinate clause
see **clause**.

subordinating conjunction
see **conjunction**.

subordination
making one clause in a sentence dependent on another.

suffix
an addition placed at the end of a word to form a derivative: e.g., *prepare – prepara*tion; *sing – sing*ing (cf. **prefix**).

synonym
a word with the same dictionary meaning as another word: e.g., *begin* and *commence*.

syntax
sentence construction; the grammatical relations of words.

tense
the time reference of verbs.

theme
a recurring or dominant idea.

thesis statement
a one-sentence assertion that gives the central argument of an essay or thesis.

topical sentence
the sentence in a paragraph (usually at the start) that expresses the main or controlling idea.

transition word
a word that shows the logical relation between sentences or parts of a sentence and thus helps to signal the change from one idea to another: e.g., *therefore, also, accordingly.*

transitive verb
one that takes an object: e.g., *hit, bring, cover.*

usage
accepted practice.

verb
that part of a predicate expressing an action, state of being, or condition, telling what a subject is or does. Verbs inflect to show tense (time). The principal parts of a verb are the three basic forms from which all tenses are made: the base infinitive, the past tense, and the past participle.

verbal
a word that is similar in form to a verb but does not function as one: a participle, a gerund, or an infinitive.

voice
the form of a verb that shows whether the subject acted (active voice) or was acted upon (passive voice: e.g., *He* **hit** *the ball* (active). *The ball* **was hit** *by him* (passive). Only transitive verbs (verbs taking objects) can be passive.

Index